RESTORATIVE JUSTICE IN THE BIBLE

Dr. Maxwell Shimba

INTRODUCTION

It's important to note that Bible Restorative Justice is primarily applied within faith communities or organizations that adopt a Christian perspective. It may not be applicable or suitable in secular or diverse settings, where different belief systems and principles of justice are at play. This approach is rooted in Christian theology and ethics, and its implementation can vary based on specific interpretations of biblical teachings and traditions.

Restorative justice is an evolution of the criminal justice system in many African and Asian countries. Traditionally, the main actors of a typical criminal justice system "retributive" would be the authority and the offenders.

Restorative justice programs in many countries initially handled cases of minor offenses such as family disputes, mischief, assaults, and theft (Ministry of Public Safety and Solicitor General, 2009). However, now they are considered for serious crimes such as rapes, and violent crimes. Being documented as effective in preventing recidivism (Umbreit, Coates, & Roberts, 2000; Umbreit, Coates, & Vos, 2004), the practice has gained acceptance worldwide and being utilized in a few countries such as New Zealand (Galaway, 1995; Maxwell & Liu, 2006), South Africa (Venter & Rankin, 2006), and in the Europe (Hydle, 2008).

A precursor that became the basis of restorative justice was a practice called dispute resolution, where two parties of conflict would meet and have a face-to-face resolution with mediation, without the involvement of the court (Doerner & Lab, 2012). This practice, then, became well-received by the public, leading to an approval by manyparties, including the legal system itself – mostly because this way, one case resolved through dispute resolution, there would be one less case to be contended by the court.

Mediation, then, became a popular choice of conflict resolution. This is the idea that the advocators of restorative justice want to employ, it is that the offenders are directly accountable to their victims, rather than being judged by an indifferent legal system. The acknowledgement of victims' rights also contributed to what became thebasis of restorative justice initiated in the United States (Shapland, Willmore, & Duff,1985; Austin/Travis County Victims' Services Task Force, 2005; Karmen, 2007).

Victim/Offender Mediation

Victim offender mediation is a process that provides interested victims an opportunity to meet their offender, in a safe and structured setting, and engage in a mediated discussion of the crime.With the assistance of a trained mediator, the victim is able to tell the offender about the crime's physical, emotional, and financial impact; to receive answers to lingering questions about the crime and the offender; and to be directly involved in developing a restitution plan for the offender to pay back his or her financial debt.

This process is different from mediation as it is practiced in civil or commercial disputes, since the involved parties are not "disputants" nor of similar status — with one an admitted offender and the other the victim. Also, the process is not primarily focused upon reaching a settlement, although most sessions do, in fact, result in a signed restitution agreement. Because of these fundamental differences with standard mediation practices, some programs call the process a victim offender "dialogue," "meeting," or "conference."

Currently, there are more than 290 victim offender mediation programs in the United States andmore than 500 in Europe. The American Bar Association recently endorsed victim offender mediation and recommends its use throughout the country. A recent statewide survey of victim service providers in Minnesota found that 91 percent of those surveyed believe that victim offender mediation should be available in every judicial district, since it represents an important victim service.

Goals:

The goals of victim-offender mediation include:

- Support the healing process of victims, by providing a safe and controlled setting for them to meet and speak with the offender on a strictly voluntary basis.
- Allow the offender to learn about the impact of the crime on the victim and to take direct responsibility for their behavior.
- Provide an opportunity for the victim and offender to develop a mutually acceptable planthat addresses the harm caused by the crime.

Implementation:

Cases may be referred to victim offender mediation programs by judges, probation officers, victimadvocates, prosecutors, defense attorneys, and police. In some programs, cases are primarily referred as a diversion from prosecution, assuming any agreement reached during the mediation session is successfully completed. In other programs, cases are usually referred after a formal admission of guilt has been accepted by the court, with mediation being a condition of probation (if the victim has volunteered to participate). Some programs receive case referrals at both stages. The majority of mediation sessions involve juvenile offenders, although the process is occasionally used with adults and even in very serious violent cases

In implementing any victim offender mediation program, it is critically important to maintain sensitivity to the needs of the victim. First and foremost, the mediator must do everything possible to ensure that the victim will not be harmed in any way. Additionally, the victim's participation must be completely voluntary, as should the participation of the offender. The victim should also be given choices, whenever possible, concerning decisions such as when and where the mediation session will take place, who will be present, who will speak first, etc. Cases should be carefully screened regarding the readiness of both victim and offender to participate. The mediator should conduct in person, pre-mediation sessions with both parties and make follow-up contacts, including the monitoring of any agreement reached.

Lessons Learned:

A large multi-site study (Umbreit, 1994) of victim-offender mediation programs with juvenile offender found the following:

- 3,142 cases were referred to the four study-site programs during a two-year period, with 95 percent of the mediation sessions resulting in a successfully negotiated restitution agreement to restore the victim's financial losses.
- Victims who met with their offender in the presence of a trained mediator were more likely to be satisfied (79 percent) with the justice system than similar victims who went through the normal court process (57 percent).
- After meeting the offender, victims were significantly less fearful of being revictimized.
- Offenders who met with their victims were far more likely to successfully complete their restitution obligation (81 percent) than similar offenders who did not participate in mediation (58 percent).
- Fewer offenders who participated in victim offender mediation recidivated (18 percent) than similar offenders who did not participate in mediation (27 percent); furthermore, participating offenders' subsequent crimes

tended to be less serious.

For More Information:

For additional information, contact Dr. Mark Umbreit, Center for Restorative Justice and Mediation, School of Social Work, University of Minnesota, 386 McNeal Hall, 1985 Buford Avenue, St. Paul, MN 55108, 612-624-4923.

This Restorative Justice Fact Sheet is presented by a partnership among the Office of Justice Programs, National Institute of Justice, Office for Victims of Crime, National Institute of Corrections, and Office of Juvenile Justice and Delinquency Prevention, all within the U.S. Department of Justice.

In general, restorative justice practices resolve issues involving crime without much of an adjudicating authority, whose main aim in the criminal justice system is mostly retribution or punishment of the offence (Roche, 2006; Azman & Mohammad, 2012). Other than that, the objectives of restorative justice are:

So, victims can come forward and get involve actively to resolve the conflictand make decisions along with their family, community, and of course, offenders (Christie, 1977; Wolhuter, Olley, & Denham, 2009).

So, the resolution of the conflict will focus more on restoration and reparation rather than punishment (Braithwaite, 2002; Boonin, 2008; Doerner & Lab, 2012).

So, the victims, offenders, and the community have a mediated dialogue to resolve resentment, offer apology or forgiveness, and to harness offender'ssense of accountability and remorse (Zehr & Mika, 1998; Doerner & Lab, 2012).

So, both the offenders and the victims are reintegrated back to the community (Doerner & Lab, 2012).

Programs of restorative justice are based on the objectives above. Victim Offender Mediation (VOA) is one of the finest examples of how dispute resolution and dialogue are the main components of restorative justice (Umbreit et al., 2004). VOA was initially a practice that existed outside the formal system, which means that government had nothing to do with the implementation of the program (Wolhuter et al., 2009). But then,finance became an issue and VOA was considered to be put in a formal system where government could be involved.

Research on the effectiveness of VOA is focused on the benefits for both offenders and victims. A meta-analysis by Bradshaw,

Roseborough, and Umbreit, (2006) found that victims generally felt satisfied with the outcome, the recidivism rate was down by 34%, and both offenders and victims felt that the processes were fair. The documented effects of VOA are argued to be related to the empowering components that it has on both offenders and victims (Choi, Green, & Kapp, 2010), which then led to numerous social workers to pay attention on how VOA can be parallel with the missions and goals of the field of social work.

Expanding the design of victim-offender mediation, family group conferences (FGC) involve wider scale of respondents: including the families of both victims and offenders (Umbreit & Zehr, 1996; Mutter, Shemmings, Dugmore, & Hyare, 2008).

FGC's were, and still are, practiced by Maori people in New Zealand (Marshall, 1999; Van Ness & Strong, 2010). Mutter and Dugmore's (2008) evaluation on several family group conferences found that all respondents viewed it as positive. Although the uses of FGS's are mostly for child offenders, but the effectiveness of this program on adult offender has been documented too (Malmberg-Heimonen, 2011).

Other programs of restorative justice that are community-oriented exist such as referral orders and reparation orders (Wolhuter et al., 2009). Community service is one of the programs where offenders are brought to an agreement and he or she needs to take the reparation of the damage resulting from the crime committed to a wider scale – which is the community. Although less focusing on the role of victims, the focus of these programs to undo the harm of the crime committed by the offenders makes it considerable to be listed down under restorative dogma.

DR. MAXWELL SHIMBA

BIBLICAL RESTORATIVE JUSTICE

What is Biblical Restorative Justice?

Biblical Restorative Justice is a framework for justice that is grounded in the teachings of the Bible, and emphasizes the importance of repairing harm caused by wrongdoing, reconciling relationships, and restoring wholeness to individuals and communities. It is based on the idea that justice is not just about punishing offenders, but also about healing and restoring both victims and offenders.

Restorative justice seeks to address the root causes of conflict and harm, and to bring about a transformation in the lives of both the victim and the offender. It is based on the belief that all individuals are created in the image of God and have inherent dignity and worth, and that justice should be focused on restoring that dignity and worth.

Restorative justice is practiced through processes such as victim-offender mediation, community conferencing, and family group conferencing, which bring together those affected by a crime or conflict to talk about the harm that has been done and to find ways to repair that harm. This approach seeks to promote healing, forgiveness, and reconciliation, and to create a sense of community ownership and responsibility for justice.

Biblical Restorative Justice is based on a number of key principles, including:

1. The importance of community: Restorative justice is grounded in the belief that individuals are interconnected and that communities have an important role to play in promoting justice and healing.
2. The value of relationships: Restorative justice emphasizes the importance of repairing relationships that have been damaged by wrongdoing, and seeks to create opportunities for dialogue and understanding between victims and offenders.
3. The need for accountability: Restorative justice recognizes the importance of holding offenders accountable for their actions, while also providing them with opportunities to take responsibility for repairing the harm they have caused.
4. The importance of healing and restoration: Restorative justice focuses on restoring wholeness to individuals and communities

that have been impacted by crime or conflict, and seeks to promote healing, forgiveness, and reconciliation.

Thus, Biblical Restorative Justice is an approach to justice that seeks to promote healing, reconciliation, and restoration, and is grounded in the belief that all individuals are created in the image of God and have inherent dignity and worth.

Biblical restorative justice implementation

Implementing Biblical restorative justice requires a commitment to the principles and values of this approach to justice, and a willingness to engage in a process that seeks to repair harm, reconcile relationships, and restore wholeness to individuals and communities. Here are some steps that can be taken to implement Biblical restorative justice:

1. Education and Training: Educate yourself and others about the principles and values of Biblical restorative justice. This may involve attending training sessions, workshops, and seminars to learn about the concepts and processes involved in this approach.

2. Engagement with the Community: Engage with the community to build relationships and promote a sense of shared responsibility for justice. This can involve reaching out to local organizations, churches, and community leaders to promote awareness of restorative justice principles and values.

3. Development of Restorative Justice Processes: Develop restorative justice processes that are appropriate for your community and the specific circumstances of each case. This may involve implementing victim-offender mediation programs, community conferencing, or other forms of restorative justice that promote dialogue and understanding between victims and offenders.

4. Establishment of Support Systems: Establish support systems for both victims and offenders. This may involve providing counseling, mentorship, or other forms of support to help individuals process the harm that has been done and to promote healing and restoration.

5. Integration with the Justice System: Integrate restorative justice principles and practices with the broader justice system. This may involve collaborating with law enforcement, courts, and other justice system stakeholders to promote the use of restorative justice in appropriate cases.

6. Evaluation and Improvement: Evaluate the effectiveness of restorative justice processes and make improvements as needed. This may involve monitoring outcomes such as victim satisfaction, offender recidivism rates, and community relations, and making adjustments to the restorative justice approach as needed.

Accordingly, implementing Biblical restorative justice requires a commitment to building relationships, promoting healing, and restoring wholeness to individuals and communities. This approach to justice requires a shift in mindset and a willingness to prioritize repairing harm over punishment and retribution.

CHAPTER I
WHAT IS RESTORATIVE JUSTICE?

What is Restorative Justice?

Restorative justice is an approach to problem solving that, in its various forms, involves the victim, the offender, their social networks, justice agencies and the community, while, restorative justice programs are based on the fundamental principle that criminal behavior not only violates the law, but also injures victims and the community. Any efforts to address the consequences of criminal behavior should, where possible, involve the offender as well as these injured parties, while also providing help and support that the victim and offender require.

Accordingly, restorative justice's method of operating "modus operandi praxis" is not one-size-fits-all and may weave traditional justice procedures "retributive" into the process. The methodologies and goals of Restorative Justice may shift depending on whether the survivor's "victim's" goals include a continued relationship with the abuser "offender". Other factors influencing how parties plan their restorative justice practices happen might include their housing situation, whether they have any children, and whether their finances are tied together like owning a property together. Face-to-face restorative justice methods such as Victim Offender Mediation must be continuously consensual on both parties "the victim and offender". If either survivor or offender determines they are no longer willing to continue the process for any reason, then the process must end. Some restorative justice scholars argue that only the victim's participation must be voluntary; however, involuntary participation by the offender could stunt accountability.

Restorative practices often involve facilitated discussions in ternary varieties: Victim Offender Mediation, family group conferences, and circle processes. Victim Offender Mediation is the most widely used method within restorative practices and has been shown to provide high rates of satisfaction among all parties. Apostle Paul used these techniques by making Onesimus, Philemon, and the Church to meet and resolve the issues between Onesimus and Philemon – Philemon Chapter 1

Verse 10-14. 10 I beseech thee for my son Onesimus, whom I have begotten in my bonds: 11which in time past was to thee unprofitable, but now profitable to thee and to me: 12 whom I have sent again: thou therefore receive him, that is, mine own bowels: 13 whom I would have retained with me, that in thy stead he might have ministered unto me in the bonds of the gospel: 14but without thy mind would I do nothing; that thy benefit should not be as it were of necessity, but willingly.

Paul announces his intention to send Onesimus directly back to Philemon and describes Onesimus as his very own affections, which expresses his deep personal love and affection for Philemon's runaway slave.

This description would serve to further soften the blow of coming into contact with Onesimus and serve to bring about a reconciliation between the two and assuage any anger Philemon might have towards his slave. Romans 12:10. Be devoted to one another in love.

Honor one another above yourselves

Victim Offender Mediation differs from traditional mediation in that "mediation does not presume a harm causing party and a harmed party," while Victim Offender Mediation and other restorative justice methods are in fact predicated on the harm caused to one party by another party. Restorative conferences should be combined with other restorative practices to create an appropriate plan to heal and re store each party to an offense.

Therefore, Victim Offender Mediation process or proceedings for resolving crime (an action or omission that constitutes an offense that may be prosecuted by the state and is punishable by law) by focusing on redressing the harm done to the victims, holding offenders accountable for their actions and, often also, engaging the community in the resolution of that conflict is called "restorative justice".

Participation of the parties is an essential part of the process that emphasizes relationship building, reconciliation and the development of agreements around a desired outcome between victims and offender. Restorative justice processes can be adapted to various cultural contexts and the needs of different communities. Through them, the victim, the offender and the community regain some control over the process. Furthermore, the process itself can often transform the relationships between the community and the justice system as a whole.

Micah 6:8 He has showed you, O man, what is good. And what does the LORD require of you? To act justly and to love mercy and to walk humbly with your God. (New International Version)

God is expecting us to act justly, which raises the questions, "What is justice", and "What does it mean to act justly?" These are some of the questions we will explore in this book.

While justice can be used to talk about retributive justice in which a person is punished for their wrongdoings, most of the time the Bible uses the word justice to refer to restorative justice, in which those who are unrightfully hurt or wronged are restored and given back what was taken from them as it is impeccable exhibited in the Book of Philemon- Read my Book – Runaway Slave.

Restorative justice is an approach to understanding and responding to crime. In terms of understanding crime, restorative justice theory emphasizes crime as harm to people, relationships, and communities. In terms of responding to crime, restorative justice practice focuses on repairing the harm inflicted by crime on people, relationships, and communities, and on giving those directly affected by the crime the opportunity to determine what that repair will look like.

Restorative justice practices incorporate several key principles or values:

Encounter – those involved in and affected by a crime should have opportunity to encounter or engage each other personally in response to it;

Inclusion – all of those involved in and affected by a crime should be included in the response, to it to the extent they want to be involved;

Amends – an offender should have opportunity to make amends, symbolical and material, for the harm caused by his or her actions; and

Reintegration – the response to a crime should seek full integration of the offender and the victim into their communities.

In its fullest and best sense, restorative justice is a binary way of seeing crime correctly and a way of responding to crime appropriately.

In the studies which follow, we will have opportunity to explore carefully the meaning and practice of restorative justice. In faith, hope, and love, may we ask God for grace to grow so that at the end of the week, and beyond, we can do better what God requires of us to act justly, to love mercy, and to walk humbly with him.

Isaiah 32:16-20

Justice will dwell in the desert and righteousness live in the fertile field.

The fruit of righteousness will be peace; the effect of righteousness will be quietness and confidence forever.

My people will live in peaceful dwelling places, in secure homes, in undisturbed places of rest.

Though hail flattens the forest and the city is leveled completely, how blessed you will be, sowing your seed by every stream, and letting your cattle and donkeys' range free. (New International Version)

Hosea 2:18-20

In that day I will make a covenant for them with the beasts of the field and the birds of the air and the creatures that move along the ground.

Bow and sword and battle I will abolish from the land, so that all may lie down in safety.

I will betroth you to me forever; I will betroth you in righteousness and justice, in love and compassion.

I will betroth you in faithfulness, and you will acknowledge the Lord.

(New International Version)

Reflection on justice:

In the passages from Isaiah and Hosea we see a picture of justice. Rich in imagery and meaning, the passages piece together a mosaic of justice using terms such as peace, security, rest, confidence, love, compassion, commitment, faithfulness, and fruitfulness. Justice is connected with right relationships among people and in all of creation. It provides a strong foundation for overcoming adversity and conflict.

Compare Isaiah and Hosea with the commonly accepted notion that justice means each person gets his or her due. For example, honest work and responsible living merit appropriate rewards in terms of standard of living and place in the community. Wrongful behaviors deserve punishment in proportion to how bad they were as defined by social codes, rules, or laws. In either case, justice means a person ought to receive what is due based on the kind or amount of good or bad he or she has done.

In other words, conversations about justice today typically emphasize the following:

Enforcement of laws

The role of the state or civil officials

Unbiased and impartial judges

Individual actions, and what is due and proportionate in response to them (i.e., fairness and equity of response in terms of what individual actions deserve or merit)

A backward-looking perspective to settle accounts from past wrong. According to the Basic Principles, a "restorative outcome" is an agreement reached as a result of a restorative process. The agreement may include referrals to programs such as reparation, restitution and community services, "aimed at meeting the individual and collective needs and responsibilities of the parties and achieving the reintegration of the victim and the offender". It may also be combined with other measures in cases involving serious offences.

As important as those are, Biblical passages such as Isaiah 32, Hosea 2, and others, provide a much larger vision of justice. That vision focuses on people, on individual and social well-being – specifically, on people in right relationship with God and with each other. Biblical justice is fundamentally personal and relational. Moreover, it envisions a full- ness of life for all.

Thus, Biblical justice emphasizes the following:

People and relationships

The well-being of people and relationships

Repair of harm to people and relationships

A forward-looking perspective to restore people and relationships in both present and future states

The Biblical conception of justice is rooted in and stems from the vision of shalom. The Hebrew word for peace, shalom (שלום) is derived from a root denoting wholeness or completeness, and its frame of reference throughout Jewish literature is bound up with the notion of shelemut, perfection.

Its significance is thus not limited to the political domain to the absence of war and enmity or to the social to the absence of quarrel and strife. It ranges over several spheres and can refer in different contexts to bounteous physical conditions, to a moral value, and, ultimately, to a cosmic principle and divine attribute.

Shalom in the Bible is a richly textured idea. Generally translated as peace, shalom means more than a lack of conflict. It envisions people in active, right, fruitful relationships with each other, with God and with creation. Peace in this sense not only reduces or prevents conflict but it also fosters individual and social well-being. It yields a fullness of life for all.

Justice then, biblically understood, seeks shalom. When wrongdoing occurs between people, shalom suffers and it is unjust to leave unresolved both the wrongdoing and the resulting harm. Practicing justice rebuilds and increases shalom for the affected individuals and society.

Accordingly, restorative justice is an attempt to respond to wrong- doers and to the harm they have caused so that relationships within the community are strengthened, injuries are resolved, community values are upheld, and victims are protected.

Biblical dual views of Restorative and Retributive Justice:

What does the Bible say should be the result if a master strikes the eye of a servant and because of it, he/she goes blind? (Exodus 21:26-27):

He shall let him go free for his eye's sake.

Note that the principle of eye for an eye has a different application for servants. The servant, if injured by the master, received something more precious than an eye - his freedom.

However, in Matthew 5:38-39, Jesus recommended: But I say unto you, that ye resist not evil: but whosoever shall smite thee on thy right cheek, turn to him the other also.

When a person insults us (slaps you on the right cheek) our first reaction is to want to give them back what they gave to us, PLUS more. Jesus said we should patiently bear such insults and offences, and not resist an evil person who insults us this way. Instead, we should trust God to defend us.

In contrast, Retributive Justice as we see in common laws and Courts, before pronouncing sentence, the judge enumerated the usual goals of sentences:

a): the need for retribution, b): the need to isolate offenders from society, c): the need to rehabilitate, d): the need to deter.

As we will learn in this book, the judge did not include the goal of restoration. Restoration is a sentencing goal that seeks to address this damage done by making the victim, the community, and even the offender whole again.

Spending time in prison or jail always has profound effects on a young person's future. Many youths, once in the prison system, will stay there for significant portions of their lives. About one-third of all people incarcerated when young return to jail or prison within a few years after release. In addition, if they do manage to stay out of prison, youth who have been incarcerated experience diminished income in comparison with their non-incarcerated peers.

In many cases, most judges as they pronounced their sentence say words similar to this: The Judge admonished the offender, "I trust that there you will forget the patterns of behavior which led to this violent offense. Is this typically the result when a youth is thrust into the prison system for years on end?

Those entering prison while still children must cope with solitary confinement, increased risk of suicide, denied adequate mental health care, and the ever-present sexual, verbal, and physical abuse. Some spend years only fleeting human contact, rather than learning to interact with others properly.

Though these offenders are incarcerated, but the time in prison is not changing them, because they miss what the Defendant attorney suggested which in many occasions changes these individuals.

Instead of this being a confrontation between two individuals regarding restitution, the legal process and the media highlighted the actions of the criminal and only secondarily remembered the victim which is all too often the case in today's legal system.
Finally:

Restorative justice, as practiced in many communities in the world, is a conflict resolution paradigm that brings together the victims, offenders, and community members to address and resolve a crime or a dispute. It aims at restoration, reparation, reintegration, and community participation in tackling crime, disputes, and related problems that affect them.

Restoration takes many forms, such as compensation, reparation or apology, and helps mend broken relationships. In Africa and Asia, this makes perfect sense because peoples tend to live communally and abhorred anything that could strain relationships, disconnect an individual or family with the community, and paralyze their social relationships.

CHAPTER II
THE VICTIM

The Victim:

A victim is defined as a person who has suffered physical or emotional harm, property damage, or economic loss as a result of a crime. The rights are available to a victim who is in the United States or who is an American citizen or permanent resident.

The following people can exercise a victim's rights if the victim is dead or not able to act on his or her own behalf:

- A victim's spouse
- A common-law partner who has lived with the victim for at least one year prior to the victim's death
- A relative or dependant of the victim
- Anyone who has custody of the victim or of the victim's dependant

A person who has been charged, convicted, or found not criminally responsible due to a mental disorder for the offence that resulted in the victimization is not defined as a victim. For example, if a parent has been charged with abuse of a child, that parent will not be allowed to exercise the child victim's rights or their own rights as a parent.

A victim's role in the criminal justice system:

The role of a victim in the criminal justice system can vary depending on the jurisdiction and the specific circumstances of the case. However, there are several rights and responsibilities that victims have in the criminal justice system, which may include:

1. The right to be informed: Victims have the right to be informed about the criminal justice process and their role in it. This includes being notified about court proceedings, plea bargains, and the outcome of the case.
2. The right to be heard: Victims have the right to express their views and concerns during the criminal justice process, including providing a victim impact statement at sentencing.
3. The right to protection: Victims has the right to protection from threats, intimidation, and harassment related to the criminal justice process.

4. The right to restitution: Victims have the right to receive restitution for any financial losses or damages they have suffered as a result of the crime.
5. The right to participate: Victims may have the opportunity to participate in the criminal justice process, such as through victim-offender mediation or restorative justice programs.
6. The responsibility to cooperate: While victims are not required to cooperate with law enforcement or prosecutors, their cooperation can be essential to the successful prosecution of the case.
7. The responsibility to report: Victims have a responsibility to report crimes to law enforcement to help prevent further harm to themselves or others.

It is important to note that the criminal justice system can be a challenging and often frustrating experience for victims, and they may require support and resources to help them navigate the process. Victim advocates and victim service providers can provide information, support, and referrals to help victims cope with the aftermath of a crime and participate in the criminal justice process.

Although a victim of crime is not a party in criminal proceedings, they play a vital role in the criminal justice process. Their testimony is a very important part of the prosecutor's case against the accused.

Legally, a victim of crime is defined as someone who has suffered from palpable harm. In some cases, this harm may be physical or emotional. However, harm can also be considered as property damage or economic loss. Not everyone who has suffered from harm is a victim in the criminal justice system.

Leviticus 19:17-18

Do not hate your brother in your heart. Rebuke your neighbor frankly so you will not share in his guilt. Do not seek revenge or bear a grudge against one of your people, but love your neighbor as yourself. I am the Lord. (New International Version)

Matthew 5:7, 9

Blessed are the merciful, for they will be shown mercy.... Blessed are the peacemakers, for they will be called sons of God. (New International Version).

Matthew 18:15-16

If your brother sins against you, go and show him his fault, just between the two of you. If he listens to you, you have won your brother

over. But if he will not listen, take one or two others along, so that every matter may be established by the testimony of two or three witnesses. (New International Version)
Galatians 6:1a

Brothers, if someone is caught in a sin, you who are spiritual should restore him gently. (New International Version)

As we have seen, a restorative justice understanding of crime focuses on the people and relationships involved in and affected by criminal wrong- doing. Crime is more than breaking a law or laws. It also harms people, communities, and relationships.

It follows then that a restorative justice response to crime focuses on people and relationships. Such a response seeks to provide opportunities for offenders, victims, families, friends, and community members to meet –to encounter each other to discuss and deal with crime and its effects on them and their relationships.

All of this is deeply in alignments with Biblical tenets and practices for responding to wrongdoing. Compare the passages from Leviticus 19, Matthew 5 and 18, and Galatians 6 and the Book of Philemon. God acknowledges the harmful reality and power of wrongdoing. The texts show that God cares about victims and offenders – both parties in conflict. God wants people in conflict to do what they can to recognize the harm and its consequences and then to seek restoration and reconciliation- Read the entire Book of Philemon and see how Apostle Paul mediated between Onesimus and Philemon. The texts from Leviticus, Matthew, and Galatians suggest that this should be done through personal engagement between people who are set against each other because of wrong-doing or conflict.

Encounter, then, is one of the key principles or values in restorative justice practice. An encounter can occur directly in a meeting between the involved parties. Alternatively, it can occur indirectly through a sequence of separate meetings with the parties involved, or through letters, videos, and the like.

Matthew 18: 15 "If your brother or sister sins, go and point out their fault, just between the two of you. If they listen to you, you have won them over. 16 But if they will not listen, take one or two others along, so that 'every matter may be established by the testimony of two or three witnesses. 17 If they still refuse to listen, tell it to the church; and if they refuse to listen even to the church, treat them as you would a pagan or a tax collector.

Whatever the means, a restorative encounter process aims to accomplish the following objectives:

Bring the parties in conflict together in an interactive process (e.g., mediation, conferencing, circles, exchange of letters or messages)

Provide a venue for victims to tell their story to others, particularly to the offender.

Give offenders an opportunity to acknowledge their actions and to understand the harm they have caused.

Make space for communication and truth-telling, leading to the sharing of emotion and to understanding and empathy, and even to confession and repentance.

Come to an agreement about how to deal with the effects of the crime, especially through actions the offender will undertake.

Create the potential for rebuilding or transforming relationships.

In short, the appropriate and effective way to pursue justice and shalom after a crime is to bring together those who are involved in and affected by it in direct or indirect personal encounter.

Through encounter with each other, the parties can take ownership of their actions and their reactions. They can exercise responsibility and compassion, and seek restoration and transformation for themselves and their relationships, by dealing personally and positively with crime and its effects.

What is "frozen fear compliance"?

Frozen fear compliance happens when victims of violent crime (like victims of hijackings) frequently seem to cooperate with their oppressor when confronted by terrifying and overpowering situation.

Furthermore, many victims second-guess themselves and begin to wonder if they are responsible for what happened to them. Maybe they did not resist or even complied with the demands of the perpetrator. It is common for victims of a crime to cooperate with the perpetrator, but it is important to remember that this compliance was rooted in fear. The reality is, their compliance may have saved their lives.

What are the emotions the victims' experiences during the "recoil" phase?

The "recoil" phase, also known as the impact phase, is the immediate emotional reaction of the victim following a traumatic event or crime. During this phase, victims may experience a range of intense and often overwhelming emotions, which can include:

1. Shock: Victims may feel a sense of disbelief, numbness, or detachment from reality. They may feel like they are in a dream or that what has happened is not real.
2. Fear: Victims may feel afraid for their safety and the safety of others. They may have heightened anxiety or a sense of vulnerability.
3. Anger: Victims may feel angry at the perpetrator, at themselves, or at the world in general. They may feel like their sense of control has been taken away.
4. Guilt: Victims may feel guilty for not being able to prevent the harm that was done to them or for their perceived role in the situation.
5. Shame: Victims may feel ashamed or embarrassed about what has happened to them, and may worry about how others will perceive them.
6. Denial: Victims may deny that the harm has occurred or minimize its impact in order to cope with the overwhelming emotions.
7. Grief: Victims may experience a sense of loss or mourning for their sense of safety or for the life they had before the harm occurred.

It is important to note that the experience of the "recoil" phase can be different for each victim and can vary in intensity and duration depending on the circumstances of the harm. Victims may require different types of support and interventions to help them cope with their emotions during this phase.

Furthermore, it is important to remember that all victims of trauma (either through crime, catastrophic acts of nature, illness or war, etc.) experience these common reactions. In the initial hours or days after the event, it is common to feel disoriented, terrified, angry, vulnerable, numb and overwhelmed. Trauma victims also need to rehearse the event and to grieve the lost object (lost innocence, control over life, loved one, etc.) Guilt is also a common emotion during this phase of recovery.

The next phase that is common to all victims of trauma occurs in the days to weeks after the event and is characterized by emotional turmoil and mood swings. Intense feelings of anger, sadness, fear, anxiety, vulnerability, confusion, helplessness and depression are common. Frightening dreams may also haunt your nights.

Eventually, they move from emotional turmoil to a period of adjustment or reorganization; from being a victim to being a survivor. Their emotions stabilize and their thoughts become more organized. They will be able to problem-solve once again and stay focused and learn from the experience.

The final stage of recovery from a traumatic event occurs months later but maybe longer for some. It is signaled by a return of hope and self-confidence. While they will never forget what happened to them, they are no longer consumed by the offense and the offender.

The WHY'S and IF'S: Most victims dealt with feelings of shame and blame. They go over and over in their mind ...:

a) Why it happened,

b) Why I reacted the way I did,

c) What I could have done differently,

d) If only I had not rebuffed the offender when he/she tried to talk to me.

e) If only I had not gone out that night

f) Perhaps I was being punished for something I did

Victims often blame themselves for what happened. Are there choices victims could have made that would have protected them? Victims may be saying the following. Maybe I could have spent my life learning self-defense or could have stayed at home in bed all day. Maybe I could have lived in a different city or could never walk by themself. Victims could spend an eternity making a list of the choices that might have saved them from losing what they lost.

But the absolute bottom line is this. Only one person makes the choice to attack. There are things we can (and should!) do to protect ourselves, but the only person who can prevent an attack is the attacker him or herself.

Many victims experience intense feelings of anger at others who should have prevented it, or at God who allowed or even caused it.

The victims needed friends who would help them not to blame themself for what happened or how they have responded, who would provide support and assistance without taking over for them.

Unfortunately, however, our friends tend to avoid the subject.

Here are things people need in the initial hours after attack, and throughout the weeks and months it takes to recover. These points will be repeated within the course.

Safety - to be reassured that this will not happen again; that the offender has been caught; to feel safe in the home environment once again.

Support network - people they trust who will allow them to express their feelings without judgment. Our young woman was lacking in this area.

Information - about the perpetrator, the investigation, your rights, etc. Too often, victims don't get the information they need during the investigation, which will compound their frustration. In many cases, the victim is sidelined during the criminal justice process.

Justice - to know that the offender will pay for his/her crime; that what was done was wrong and not deserved.

Restitution - repayment for what was taken from them. Sometimes this may be material, at other times it is knowing that justice was served.

Furthermore, some of the victims even implied that they contributed to what happened and that they are somehow to blame.

In the Book of Job, his friends were equally tactless. His friend, Zophar declared Job must be wicked, or he would not be suffering like the wicked. What did Zophar say would happen to Job if he persisted in his wickedness? (Job 11:20): But the eyes of the wicked shall fail, and they shall not escape, and their hope shall be as the giving up of the ghost.

Did Job accept Zophar's assessment of his spiritual condition? (Job 12)?

In Job 15, verses 2 through 13, mentioned 8 of the 15 sins Eliphaz said Job had committed.:

a): Are you the first man who was born?
b): Or were you made before the hills?
c): Have you heard the counsel of God?
d): Do you limit wisdom to yourself?
e): What do you know that we do not know?
f): What do you understand that is not in us?

g): Are the consolations of God too small for you,

h): Why does your heart carry you away,

There is much to admire in the theology and philosophy of Job's friends. Much of what they said is generally true and valuable, and backed by the wisdom of the ancients. They believed in God's power and His absolute righteousness. They also believed that God would forgive a sinner and take him back into favor if the sinner responded correctly to the punishment God appointed.

However, the application of these deeply held beliefs about how life, God and the universe was working in Job's situation was completely wrong. The reasons for his calamities were completely beyond the understanding of Job's friends, although they were confident that they understood the situation perfectly.

Again, did Job accept Eliphaz's assessment of his spiritual condition? (Job 16):

No, Job did not accept Eliphaz's assessment of his spiritual condition. In Job chapter 16, Job responds to Eliphaz's accusations that he must have sinned and brought about his own suffering. Job argues that he is innocent and that his suffering is not a result of any wrongdoing on his part. He expresses his deep anguish and despair, and he challenges his friends' understanding of God's justice.

In particular, Job criticizes his friends for their lack of compassion and their insensitive remarks. He says, "You are miserable comforters, all of you! Will your long-winded speeches never end? What ails you that you keep on arguing?" (Job 16:2-3, NIV).

Job goes on to describe the extent of his physical and emotional pain, and he expresses his deep sense of isolation and abandonment. He says, "Even now my witness is in heaven; my advocate is on high. My intercessor is my friend as my eyes pour out tears to God; on behalf of a man, he pleads with God as one pleads for a friend" (Job 16:19-21, NIV).

Accordingly, Job's response to Eliphaz in chapter 16 is a rejection of his friends' accusations and a plea for understanding and compassion. He maintains his innocence and his faith in God, even in the midst of his suffering.

Did Job's third friend, Bildad, defend Job's innocence in the situation. (Job 18)?

No, Bildad did not defend Job's innocence in the situation. In fact, in Job chapter 18, Bildad continues to argue that Job must be guilty of some secret sin, which has brought about his suffering. He describes the fate of the wicked in vivid and terrifying language, implying that Job is being punished by God for his sins. Bildad accuses Job of being arrogant and rebelling against God, and he urges Job to repent and seek God's mercy.

Bildad's speech in chapter 18 is part of a larger dialogue in the book of Job, in which Job's friends Eliphaz, Bildad, and Zophar come to visit him after he has suffered a series of calamities. They try to comfort him, but also insist that his suffering must be a result of his own wrongdoing. Job, however, maintains his innocence and questions why God would allow him to suffer so greatly.

Thus, Bildad's argument in chapter 18 is not a defense of Job's innocence, but rather an accusation of his guilt and a call for repentance.

The experience of being a crime victim can be highly intense, touching all areas of life. Some of the ways the victim's life are impacted?

a): It affected their sleeping,

b): It affect their appetite,

c): It affects their health.

d): It makes their job performance deteriorated.

Why is crime so devastating, so difficult to recover from?

Crime can be devastating and difficult to recover from for several reasons:

1. Physical and Emotional Harm: Crime can cause physical injuries, emotional trauma, and long-term psychological harm to victims. The physical and emotional harm can affect the victim's ability to function in daily life and impact their overall well-being.

2. Financial Loss: Crime can result in financial losses for victims, such as medical expenses, lost wages, and property damage. These losses can be significant and difficult to recover from, particularly for victims who are already struggling financially.

3. Disruption of Daily Life: Crime can disrupt the victim's daily life and routines, making it difficult to maintain relationships, attend work or school, or engage in recreational activities.

4. Loss of Trust: Crime can erode the victim's trust in others, particularly if the perpetrator was someone they knew or trusted. The loss of trust can impact the victim's ability to form relationships and feel safe in their community.

5. Stigma and Shame: Victims of crime may experience feelings of shame, stigma, or blame, particularly in cases of sexual assault

or domestic violence. These feelings can be difficult to overcome and may impact the victim's willingness to seek help or support.

6. Legal Process: The criminal justice process can be lengthy and stressful for victims, particularly if they are required to testify in court or face the perpetrator. The legal process can also be confusing and overwhelming, particularly for victims who are unfamiliar with the justice system.

Hence, the impact of crime on victims can be significant and long-lasting, and recovery may require a range of support and resources. It is important for victims to seek help and support as soon as possible after a crime, and to connect with victim service providers and advocates who can provide information, resources, and support throughout the recovery process.

And this can rock our world in a variety of ways.

Physical effects:

- headaches, migraines or stomach aches
- not being able to concentrate or focus
- sleeping problems including nightmares and vivid dreams
- change in eating habits such as loss of appetite or overeating.

Emotional and psychological effects:

- anxiety, stress, worry or fear
- being angry and frustrated
- flashbacks or intrusive thoughts or going over and over in your mind what happened
- feeling no-one really understands or people don't believe you
- feelings of blame; whether others blame you for what happened or you blame yourself
- feeling vulnerable, unsafe and not being able to stay on your own
- feelings of being out of control or unable to cope
- a loss of interest or feeling disconnected from the world
- difficulty talking about the crime and how it makes you feel
- feelings of shame or humiliation
- withdrawing from relationships or social activities.

To recover, victims need to move from the "recoil" phase to a reorganization phase. In cases of serious crimes, they need to move from being victims to being survivors.

It has been suggested that to find healing, victims must find answers to six basic questions.:

a): What happened?
b): Why did it happen to me?
c): Why did I act as I did at the time?
d): Why have I acted as I have since that time?
e): What if it happens again?
f): What does this mean for me and for my outlook (my faith, my vision of the world, my future)?

Victims sense of personal autonomy has been stolen from them by an offender, and they need to have this sense of personal power returned to them.

Two things' victims can do to feel empowered again is:
a): Sense of control over their environment.
b): Sense of control or involvement in the resolution of their own cases. They need to feel that they have choices and that these choices are real.

Here are more practical tips and suggestions that have helped other victims of crime:

- Take time to think through what you need to feel safe, better, less anxious ...
- Make your own decisions about what happens next. This helps to increase your sense of control again.
- Don't expect too much of yourself right away, as you are already coping with the effects of a crime.
- Remember you are still the same person you were before the crime.
- Re-establish your normal routine as soon as possible.
- Eliminate any unnecessary stresses.
- Do something each day - big or small - to care for yourself such as exercise, seeing a friend, buying a bunch of flowers, making an appointment you need.
- Keep a journal or diary about feelings and accomplishments.
- Talk to a biblical counsellor if you are feeling overwhelmed.

Victims also need to feel justice was served. In the process, they need:
a): Victims need assurance that what happened to them was wrong, unfair, undeserved.
b): They need opportunities to speak the truth of what happened to them, including their suffering.
c): They need to be heard and affirmed.
d): Victims need to know that steps are being taken to rectify the

wrong and to reduce the opportunities for it to recur.

e): They may want restitution, not just for the material recovery involved but for the moral statement implied in the recognition that the act was wrongful and in the attempt to make things right.

Furthermore, the key rights should include:

- the right to be kept informed about the case by the police (at least monthly)
- the right to hear when a suspect is arrested, charged, bailed or sentenced
- the right to apply for extra help when giving evidence in court, if the victim feels vulnerable or intimidated
- the right to be told when an offender is going to be released, if they have been sentenced for a violent or sexual offence.

It would seem logical, given all this, that victims would be at the center of the justice process, with their needs as a major focus, however, the reality with regard to the victim's needs in the process of serving justice are frequently astonished to find that charges can be either pursued or dropped without regard to victims' wishes and that they are provided little information about the case.

Such neglect of victims not only fails to meet their needs; it compounds the injury. Worst of all, from the point of view of the victim, the lack of including them in the justice process leaves them with a lack of resolution.

Below are some of the things a victim should be kept informed about, as his/her case is investigated and brought to court.

a): Their complained has been heard

b): The offender is been prosecuted. Charges are been pressed.

c): The victims needs are being attended

d): Justice will be served

At the end of the process, many victims have come to court expecting that the trial will be a time when everything they have been through will be resolved and made right. If the accused is found not guilty, that will come as a huge disappointment. Even if the accused is found guilty and the victim is happy with the sentence, the time after a trial may still feel like an anticlimax. And the victim will still have to cope with all the problems the crime caused in his/her life.

CHAPTER III
THE OFFENDER

The Offender

Offender is a legal term used in the context of criminal law to refer to a person convicted of committing a crime or offense. An adult offender is a person convicted of committing a crime after reaching the legal age of majority. There are 30 most important Bible scriptures on offense. Good sense makes one slow to anger, and it is his glory to overlook an offense. A brother offended is more unyielding than a strong city, and quarreling is like the bars of a castle.

Acts 25:11 "For if I be an offender, or have committed anything worthy of death, I refuse not to die: but if there be none of these things whereof these accuse me, no man may deliver me unto them. I appeal unto Caesar."

Isaiah 29:21 "That make a man an offender for a word, and lay a snare for him that reproveth in the gate, and turn aside the just for a thing of nought."

There are different types of criminals which are classified as under.

- Habitual criminal. ...
- Legalistic criminals. ...
- Moralistic criminals. ...
- Psychopathic criminals. ...
- Institutional criminals or white color criminals. ...
- Situational or occasional criminals. ...
- Professional criminals. ...
- Organized criminals.

Who is the offender in law?

A person who is guilty of a crime: first-time/repeat/habitual offender A first-time offender might expect probation rather than a jail sentence. convicted/alleged offenders.

Is it a legal offense?

The definition of legal offense in the dictionary is a crime that breaks a particular law and requires a particular punishment.

Deuteronomy 19:15 One witness is not enough to convict a man accused of any crime or offense he may have committed. A matter must be established by the testimony of two or three witnesses. (New International Version)

Matthew 18:15-17 If your brother sins against you, go and show him his fault, just between the two of you. If he listens to you, you have won your brother over. But if he will not listen, take one or two others along, so that every matter may be established by the testimony of two or three witnesses. If he refuses to listen to them tell it to the church; and if he refuses to listen even to the church, treat him as you would a pagan or a tax collector. (New International Version)

1 Timothy 5:19 Do not entertain an accusation against an elder unless it is brought by two or three witnesses. (New International Version)

Crime fundamentally involves harm to people and relationships. Appropriate and effective response to crime brings people together, directly or indirectly, to deal with the crime and its effects. This is the beginning of a restorative response to crime. All of those involved in and affected by a crime should be invited to participate in this process. In many discussions of restorative justice, those affected by a crime are called "stakeholders." Inclusion of all stakeholders is one of the key principles or values of restorative justice practices in seeking to move forward from the harm caused by crime.

In many Biblical texts, such as the ones above, we see the critical importance of including all concerned people – all stakeholders – in dealing with wrongdoing. Conflict, wrongdoing, and crime alienate and isolate people emotionally and relationally – in addition to the material or physical damages they cause. It is right and good to respond to conflict by including as many as necessary among those affected.

Inclusion can take various forms. One way is through full sharing by justice officials of information about proceedings and resources with all affected parties, especially with victims, families and friends, and communities. Another form might be to allow victims to be present in court, to offer victim impact statements, and perhaps even grant them legal standing during the criminal proceedings. Restorative justice practice has suggested other ways to include the stakeholders, such as the various kinds of family or community gatherings to address wrong- doing or conflict (e.g., conferencing and circles). The parties can be included at various points throughout the process: investigation; pre-sentencing; plea bargaining; trial; sentencing; and post-sentencing.

We should not expect that inclusion of affected parties is necessarily a simple and easy component in seeking a restorative response to crime. Not all may see inclusion as a value. Some victims may balk at participating in a process that involves encounter with the offender. Participants may be strongly disposed to pursue their own perspectives, needs, and interests at the expense of others, at the expense of trying to resolve the conflict and harm.

Yet inclusion is a key value in addressing wrongdoing and crime in the following ways and for the following reasons, perhaps especially forvictims.

Inclusion, negatively put, means an affected person is not beingignored.

Inclusion, positively put, means an affected person participates, takes or gains responsibility, shares his or her perspectives and feelings and needs, and influences the outcome.

Inclusive, collaborative processes, negatively put, reduce the prospect of one party dominating the shape of the outcome.

Inclusive, collaborative processes, positively put, bring in other parties who may be helpful in resolving the conflict.

Inclusive processes are collaborative, involving all parties in the conflict who wish to participate.

Inclusive, collaborative processes allow all parties to listen to each other and understand each other as far as possible.

Inclusion of all stakeholders in the process of addressing a crime can reduce the feelings of increased alienation and isolation through being discounted or ignored by the response to a problem. Even more, inclusion can help to overcome the experience of alienation and isolation. It can bring together as many as necessary in efforts to try to address restoratively as many aspects as possible of the material, personal, and social damages caused by crime.

Why throughout the legal process, most of the decisions have been made for the offender by others? (Prosecutor, judge, probation officers, psychiatrists)

Throughout the legal process, it is true that many decisions are made for the offender by others. The criminal justice system is designed to hold offenders accountable for their actions and to protect the rights of victims and the community. As a result, offenders may not have as much control over the decisions that are made about their case as they would in other situations.

For example, after an arrest, the decision about whether to charge the offender with a crime is typically made by the prosecutor, not the offender. The offender may be able to negotiate a plea deal or go to trial, but ultimately the decision about the outcome of the case will be made by the judge or jury. If the offender is found guilty, the judge will sentence them according to the law, which may limit their options for punishment or rehabilitation.

However, it is important to note that offenders do have some agency in the legal process. They have the right to choose their own attorney and to participate in their own defense. They may also be able to negotiate a plea deal or to request a particular sentence from the judge.

Moreover, there are alternative approaches to justice, such as restorative justice, that prioritize the involvement of all parties, including the offender, in the decision-making process. Restorative justice seeks to repair the harm caused by the crime and to promote healing and reconciliation, rather than simply punishing the offender. In such cases, the offender may have a more active role in the process of making decisions and finding a resolution that addresses the needs of all parties involved.

Prison is the normal response to crime. Judges find it necessary to explain and rationalize the sentence other than prison.:

Instead of learning nonviolent patterns of behavior while in prison, the offenders will learn that:
a): The conflict is normal,
b): That violence is the great problem solver,
c): That one must be violent in order to survive,
d): That one responds to frustration with violence.

California allows youth offenders as young as 14 to be transferred from the juvenile system to adult courts. Most of the teenagers who are tried as adults and sentenced to life in adult institutions are placed in Level 4 maximum-security prisons. Although these are designed to handle inmates that cannot or should not be housed with the general population of inmates, along with teens you will find inmates who are validated prison gang members, gang bosses or shot callers - and these are extremely violent.

The offenders age and small physical stature make it likely that he/she will become the victim of not just violence but sexual violence.

In addition, young prisoners are more susceptible to negative influences than adults. Facing the reality of their lengthy sentence and potentially never going home, young offenders seek protection and try to fit in somewhere in their new world. Because a juvenile's identity is still developing, he or she can potentially adopt negative behaviors that are the norm in a hostile prison environment. What an extremely, destructive effect on a young adult's life.

Rape is often not actually motivated by prolonged sexual deprivation. Instead, motivations for rape may include:
a): for expressing contempt and for degrading others.
b): understandings of masculinity and femininity.

The typical emotional repercussions for young men who go through such an experience are self-worth and manhood will be severely damaged and distorted by this experience.

Instead of being in a situation where the young man will learn nonviolent ways to handle conflict, he will be spending at least 20 years in an atmosphere which nourishes and teaches violence.

Violence will probably become a way of coping, a way of solving problems, and a way of communicating.

Wherefore, Young prisoners overwhelmed by feelings of helplessness and hopelessness cannot focus on changing their thinking and behavior, because they are focused on how to survive. How can rehabilitation be possible in such a dangerous environment?
Much crime and violence are simply a way of asserting personal identity and power.

The fear of being victimized or assaulted produces a need for security, which leads many young prisoners to rely on gangs, weapons, and violence for survival.

The violence of most violent men is ultimately spawned by the hostility and abuse of others, and it feeds on low self-confidence and fractured self-esteem.

The entire prison setting is structured to dehumanize in the following ways:
a): Prisoners are given numbers,
b): standardized clothing,
c): and little or no personal space

Teenagers in adult prisons often end up in solitary, either because they are considered disciplinary problems, because they feel compelled to join prison gangs, or because they have to be isolated from adult offenders for their own protection.

The focus of the entire prison setting is on obedience, on learning to take orders. The prisoner has 3 possible choices:

a): He or she can learn to obey,

b): to be submissive.

c): or learn not to obey

During the prison experience, our young offender will learn to be dependent.:

a) He will not pay rent,

b) He will not have to manage money,

c) He will not be primarily responsible for a family.

d) He will be dependent upon the state to take care of him.

In prison, young convict will learn that domination is the key to interpersonal relationships, whether over ...:

a): whether over a marriage partner,

b): a friend,

c): or a business acquaintance.

Caring will be seen as **a** weakness.

Actually, this is an issue outside of prison as well as inside. Kindness is a strength when you help someone who truly is in need and deserves it. But it is definitely a weakness if you offer acts of kindness to people who are simply trying to manipulate you. Others will see you as weak and spineless, and will try to take advantage of you.

In Ephesians 4:32 the Apostle Paul told us: "And be ye kind one to another, tenderhearted, forgiving one another, even as God for Christ's sake hath forgiven you." The believer should seek to show the same kindness, tender heartedness and forgiveness to others that God has shown him. If we treat others as God treats us, we will fulfill everything Paul told us to do in this chapter. Pray for wisdom and discernment through the guidance of the Holy Spirit as you shower people with your acts of kindness.

For this judge, and most people today, accountability for offenders means: that the offender must experience punitive consequences—often prison—whether for deterrence or for punishment.

The criminal justice process focuses on the wrongs committed by the offender, diverting attention from the harm done to the victim.

Offenders are rarely encouraged or allowed to see the real human costs of what they have done.

Judge Dennis Challeen of district court bench in Winona, Minnesota points out that the problem with most sentences is that they make offenders accountable (in the sense of taking their punishment), but they do not make offenders responsible.

Taking full responsibility for criminal behavior requires:

• Understanding how that behavior affected other human beings (not just the courts or officials).

• Acknowledging that the behavior resulted from a choice that could have been made differently.

• Acknowledging to all affected that the behavior was harmful to others.

• Taking action to repair the harm where possible.

• Making changes necessary to avoid such behavior in the future. Sadly, the offender seldom has the opportunity to understand or fulfill all this.

While in prison, our convict will have:

a) no confront the stereo types and rationalizations that have led up to his offense.

b) no opportunity to build the interpersonal skills and the coping skills that he will need to live successfully on the outside.

c) no way to face up to what he has done or to make things right.

d) no way to way to deal with the guilt that such an offense causes.

e) and there is no place in the system where offenders can be forgiven, where he/she can feel he/she has made things right.

Given all this, what are his alternatives?

a): He can avoid the issue, rationalizing his behavior.

b): He can turn his anger on himself and contemplate suicide.

c): He can turn his anger on others.

An offender continues to be defined as an offender long after he has paid his debt to society by serving his prison term.

To summarize, nothing in the criminal justice system is likely to start him on the road to wholeness.

Now, more than 600,000 inmates are leaving state and federal prisons every year. How they fare on the outside, and how communities cooperate in absorbing these ex-inmates, is a topic of growing concern.

After years in a cell dreaming of freedom, ex-offenders are often unprepared for it. Many have minimal education and work experience and are shackled by past addictions and mental illnesses. Those who are capable of searching for a job need to find a boss who will overlook their crimes. The latest national data indicate that about two-thirds of released prisoners are rearrested within three years.

Conclusion of Chapter II and III
Victim/Offender Mediation

Victim offender mediation is a process that provides interested victims an opportunity to meet their offender, in a safe and structured setting, and engage in a mediated discussion of the crime. With the assistance of a trained mediator, the victim is able to tell the offender about the crime's physical, emotional, and financial impact; to receive answers to lingering questions about the crime and the offender; and to be directly involved in developing a restitution plan for the offender to pay back his or her financial debt.

This process is different from mediation as it is practiced in civil or commercial disputes, since the involved parties are not "disputants" nor of similar status — with one an admitted offender and the other the victim. Also, the process is not primarily focused upon reaching a settlement, although most sessions do, in fact, result in a signed restitution agreement. Because of these fundamental differences with standard mediation practices, some programs call the process a victim offender "dialogue," "meeting," or "conference."

Currently, there are more than 290 victim offender mediation programs in the United States and more than 500 in Europe. The American Bar Association recently endorsed victim offender mediation and recommends its use throughout the country. A recent statewide survey of victim service providers in Minnesota found that 91 percent of those surveyed believe that victim offender mediation should be available in every judicial district, since it represents an important victim service.

Goals:

The goals of victim offender mediation include:

- Support the healing process of victims, by providing a safe and controlled setting for them to meet and speak with the offender on a strictly voluntary basis.
- Allow the offender to learn about the impact of the crime on the victim and to take direct responsibility for their behavior.
- Provide an opportunity for the victim and offender to develop a mutually acceptable plan that addresses the harm caused by the crime.

Implementation:

Cases may be referred to victim offender mediation programs by judges, probation officers, victim advocates, prosecutors, defense attorneys, and police. In some programs, cases are primarily referred as a diversion from prosecution, assuming any agreement reached during the mediation session is successfully completed. In other programs, cases are usually referred after a formal admission of guilt has been accepted by the court, with mediation being a condition of probation (if the victim has volunteered to participate). Some programs receive case referrals at both stages. The majority of mediation sessions involve juvenile offenders, although the process is occasionally used with adults and even in very serious violent cases

In implementing any victim offender mediation program, it is critically important to maintain sensitivity to the needs of the victim. First and foremost, the mediator must do everything possible to ensure that the victim will not be harmed in any way. Additionally, the victim's participation must be completely voluntary, as should the participation of the offender. The victim should also be given choices, whenever possible, concerning decisions such as when and where the mediation session will take place, who will be present, who will speak first, etc. Cases should be carefully screened regarding the readiness of both victim and offender to participate. The mediator should conduct in person, pre-mediation sessions with both parties and make follow-up contacts, including the monitoring of any agreement reached.

Lessons Learned:

A large multi-site study (Umbreit, 1994) of victim offender mediation programs with juvenile offenders found the following:

3,142 cases were referred to the four study-site programs during a two-year period, with 95 percent of the mediation sessions resulting in a successfully negotiated restitution agreement to restore the victim's financial losses.

Victims who met with their offender in the presence of a trained mediator were more likely to be satisfied (79 percent) with the justice system than similar victims who went through the normal court process (57 percent).

After meeting the offender, victims were significantly less fearful of being revictimized.

Offenders who met with their victims were far more likely to successfully complete their restitution obligation (81 percent) than similar offenders who did not participate in mediation (58 percent).

Fewer offenders who participated in victim offender mediation recidivated (18 percent) than similar offenders who did not participate in mediation (27 percent); furthermore, participating offenders' subsequent crimes tended to be less serious.

For More Information:

For additional information, contact Dr. Mark Umbreit, Center for Restorative Justice and Mediation, School of Social Work, University of Minnesota, 386 McNeal Hall, 1985 Buford Avenue, St. Paul, MN 55108, 612-624-4923.

This Restorative Justice Fact Sheet is presented by a partnership among the Office of Justice Programs, National Institute of Justice, Office for Victims of Crime, National Institute of Corrections, and Office of Juvenile Justice and Delinquency Prevention, all within the U.S. Department of Justice.

A Comprehensive analysis of Restorative Justice Practices:

Victim Offender Mediation "Victim offender mediation is a process that provides interested victims an opportunity to meet their offender, in a safe and structured setting, and engage in a mediated discussion of the crime. With the assistance of a trained mediator, the victim is able to tell the offender about the crime's physical, emotional, and financial impact; to receive answers to lingering questions about the crime and the offender; and to be directly involved in developing a restitution plan for the offender to pay back his or her financial debt" faces numerous exegesis and challenges in Intimate Partner Violence settings. Foremost among this arduousness is the belief that the power imbalance precludes any mediation or communication between the parties. One expectation is that survivors of domestic violence are unable to reach equal bargaining power with their abusers. On the other side of the relationship, there is the fear (whether founded or unfounded) that abusers are unprepared or unwilling to take responsibility for their actions. Finally, communities themselves might present structural, cultural, or legal challenges in the face of practices that show empathy even to offenders.

These obstacles and challenges can be valid. However, a basic tenet of restorative justice methods on a practical level is the structured nature of those methods. Restorative victim-offender conferences are always facilitated by a trained, trauma-informed neutral party. Conferences are highly structured and even often scripted. Most importantly, restorative justice plans, especially ones involving victim-offender conferencing, are predicated on the safety and con- sent of all parties. Because restorative models of justice are primarily focused on healing, the practices must be individualistic and tailored to the unique needs of each survivor, offender, and community. Victim Offender Mediation is one method of many restorative practices that can be combined to offer deep and broad benefits to survivors, offender, and communities.

Survivor-Based Challenges

Some victims and/or survivors may not benefit from restorative justice practices. This may be due to a plenty of reasons as construed hereto: a sustained dynamic of the abuser's manipulations, control, and the survivor's submission; post-traumatic stress disorder or anxiety; triggering situations such as a partner's continued substance use; a painful custody battle; or simply an abuser's lack of interest in taking accountability for their actions. In those cases, Victim Offender Mediation may not be the best option and it does not have to be the best option for everyone. In fact, most restorative justice practices are amalgamated or consolidated with traditional justice practices to provide the best benefits to the involved parties. It is better for the judicial system to have innumerable paths that can benefit more people in breadth and in depth rather than funneling all parties onto one road of revictimization.

Survivors thrive and heal best when they are humanized, not paternalized.

Intimate partner

Violence (IPV) refers to violence and aggression between people in a close relationship. It can happen to men or women. There are risks, or red flags, you can look for in your partner's behavior. Learn about IPV and its effects as well as ways you can stay safe and get help. PV refers specifically to violence and aggression between intimate partners. IPV can include physical, sexual or psychological abuse or stalking. Acts of IPV range in how often they occur or how violent they are. It can happen to women or men who have intimate relationships with women, men or both. It can happen no matter your age, income, race, ethnicity, culture, religion, or disability.

IPV includes, but is not limited to, any of the following:

Physical violence: hitting, pushing, grabbing, biting, choking strangulating, shaking, slapping, kicking, hair-pulling, restraining

Sexual violence: attempted or actual sexual contact when the partner does not want to or is unable to consent (for example, when affected by alcohol or illness)

Threats of physical or sexual abuse: ways to cause fear through words, looks, actions or weapons

Psychological or emotional abuse: name calling, humiliating, putting you down, keeping you from friends and family, bullying, controlling where you go or what you wear

Stalking: following, harassing, or unwanted contact that makes you feel afraid.

Some people experience only one of these forms of violence while others experience many types of violence. IPV can be a single event or last for many years. No matter what, no one deserves to be treated this way. Source: Intimate Partner Violence - PTSD: National Center for PTSD (va.gov)

Each survivor of Inmate Partner Violence, not the person who committed the illegal act, not the community, not the legal system is the best source for determining what is best for that survivor. Survivors of Inmate Partner Violence can have greatly various goals and needs for healing from their trauma. Some survivors may not want to face their offenders and will not proceed with Victim Offender Mediation, in contrast, many victims are ready to heal and can move forward best with restorative methods, including but not limited to face-to-face facilitated conferences with their offenders. Allowing survivors to freely make that solitary decision in the first place encourages the fact of their independent agency and helps to deconstruct the abusive narrative.

Offender-Based Challenges:

One particularly momentous and serious issue revolving around Victim Offender Mediation's effectiveness and feasibility regarding perpetrators of Inmate Partner Violence the need for perpetrators to consent and admit accountability and responsibility for their actions. Restorative options rather than imprisonment, probation, or fines may encourage offenders to enter restorative practices wholeheartedly to avoid severe punishment. However, some offenders simply may be unwilling to accept accountability whatsoever. In those cases, as in cases where the survivor is unwilling to face the offender, Victim Offender Mediation may be unsuitable, and other auxiliary restorative practices, such as surrogate mediation, or traditional justice practices might be better recourse or alternatives.

Accordingly, batterers' intervention programs "Batterer Intervention Programs (BIP) are programs that batterers attend—some voluntarily, some under court order—to educate and rehabilitate the batterer. The goal of <u>BIPs</u> is to change offender thinking and behavior with the result that offenders are held accountable and victim safety is enhanced and to decrease the likelihood of further violence", which are intended to be an adjunct restorative alternative or supplement to traditional engagement in the criminal legal system, have shown discouraging results.

Batterers' intervention programs generally involve educational, feminist, and cognitive behavioral programs in a small group or circle format with other abusers, whereas other restorative practices, including victim-offender conferencing, may involve direct conferencing with the survivor with long-term counseling or follow-up afterwards. Batterers' intervention programs may place too much emphasis on the abuser without placing appropriate emphasis on the offender's impact on the victim, which gives the survivor less agency and less room to heal and discounts the need for accountability. This is patently unfair and disrespectful to victims, and in fact, federal and state victims' rights provisions often specify that victims have the right to be treated with fairness and respect.

This continued state attention on the abuser and the lack of emphasis on the impact on the survivor can reinforce the mindset that the abuser is in control, while the survivor is forgotten. Victim Offender Mediation could provide a solution to the Batterers' intervention programs problem. In contrast to the batterers' intervention programs strategy, restorative methods can offer appropriate emphasis on the offender's wrongful actions against the survivor. Victim Offender Mediation, which involves the survivor, the offender, and a facilitator and which are intentionally heavily structured, require significant time and attention devoted to the survivor's concerns. This can increase survivor satisfaction and empowerment, which "attends to the lay, rather than legal, perspectives of crime and encourages a holistic understanding of the offense."

Community-Based Challenges:

Societal attitudes "Societal attitudes are the ideas, values and beliefs held by people in a particular society. These attitudes sometimes affect the way that people behave. Behavior relates to the actions that express these ideas, values and beliefs. Societal attitudes and behaviors are constantly changing." towards gender-based violence, including Inmate Partner Violence, impact the perpetration, survivor response, and institutional responses to that gender-based violence. The same is true for societal attitudes regarding gender norms, which "can interact with structural inequalities in ways that can increase rates of [violence against women] and mute the effects of protective factors." A significant challenge within broader communities is the feeling that perpetrators of domestic violence do not deserve a chance to right their wrongs. It is this retributive community mindset and legal theory which perpetuates abusive cycles and prevents successful reintegration into the community. "The problem there is not an inability to recognize the pain inflicted, but rather a worldview that diminishes people's rights and feelings into something that can be violated, thus succumbing to a presumption toward self-interest and self-preservation."

Finally, Western society frequently perpetuates the misogynistic attitude that survivors of domestic violence somehow deserved violence, incited violence, or suffered from a mental disorder that sparked the violence. The psychiatric field, for example, historically has pathologized some traditionally "feminine" behavior as a self-defeating personality disorder. Typical diagnostic criteria of this "disorder" included choosing people and situations leading to disappointment or failure; inciting angry or rejecting responses from others and feeling hurt in response; and engaging in unsolicited self-sacrifice. "The self-defeating personality disorder has been critiqued . . . as describing as maladaptive those behaviors that battered women and other victims of interpersonal violence adopt to keep themselves from serious harm."

Some Common Themes:

The word "restore" appears 136 times throughout the books of the Bible. The most encouraging Bible scriptures on restoration. Jeremiah 30:17. "For I will restore health to you, and your wounds I will heal," declares the Lord, "because they have called you an outcast: 'It is Zion, for whom no one cares!'".

The various characteristics of existing restorative programs can be situated along a number of continuums. Existing programs vary considerably in formality; in how they associate to the criminal justice system "The criminal justice system is essentially a maze of agencies and processes that seek to control crime, minimize crime, and impose penalties for the commission of crimes. There are various levels of the criminal justice system presently operating in the United States, including the local level, state level, and federal level. Each level has its own police department. All of these agencies are police, but each are on a different governmental level in pursuit of the same objective"; how they are operated, in the level of involvement they encourage from various parties, or in the main objectives they pursue. The view consolidated in this book is that a balance must always be achieved in order to fit the circumstances within which a program is being developed (e.g., limits of the existing legal framework, limited support from criminal justice officials, cultural obstacles, limited public support, limited means).

There is also considerable variation in the extent to which criminal justice professionals participate in restorative processes. For example, the role of justice professionals in circle sentencing, with the exception of formal completion of legal tasks (e.g., prosecutor reading the charges, judge calling the session to order), is limited. While prosecutors make recommendations to the court in indictable offences and judges are asked for legal input on what is required by statute, officials for the most part become members of the circle, expressing their personal views of the offence, offender and victim when it is their turn to speak.

Although there is no perfect agreement on what constitute a "true" restorative justice approach, these are mostly matters of choices needing to be made carefully at the time of designing a new program or strategy.

A large proportion of restorative justice programs are operated by public sector organizations. There are court-based programs, police-based programs, and programs that are operated by not-for-profit organizations in the community. While public sector agencies tend to utilize professionals, community-based programs generally rely on trained volunteers from the community.

While restorative justice programs vary on a number of key dimensions, there are also a number of commonalities. These are evident in the description in the selection of programs presented below.

Common attributes of restorative justice programs are:

Crime victims are provided with an opportunity to:	Offenders are provided with an opportunity to:
Be directly involved in resolving the situation and addressing the consequences of the offence	Acknowledge responsibility for the offence and understand the effects of the offence on the victim
Receive answers to their questions about the crime and the offender	Express emotions (even remorse) about the offence
Express themselves about the impact of the offence	Receive support to repair harm caused to the victim or oneself and family
Receive restitution or reparation	Make amends or restitution/reparation
Receive an apology	Apologize to victims
Restore, when appropriate, a relationship with the offender	Restore their relationship with the victim, when appropriate
Reach closure	Reach closure

Benefits of the Restorative Justice Practices:

With restorative justice processes, success is measured not by how much punishment is given to the offender, but by how much harm has been repaired or prevented to happen again. Restorative justice offers a multitude of benefits, from the empowerment of individuals to cost savings for communities.

Benefits to victims:

Empowerment. When victims are offered the opportunity to have a safe and facilitated dialogue with the person who harmed them, they feel empowered and invested in the process. Victims' needs are acknowledged and considered, which gives them a voice in an often-impersonal system.

Meaningful dialogue. Victims are given the opportunity to explain how they were harmed, get answers to their questions, and state what they need the offender to do to make amends.

Recovery and satisfaction. Restorative justice boasts a high rate of victim satisfaction. Many are able to recover what was taken from them, whether it be material possessions or their sense of security and peace of mind. They are more likely to be able to move on from the incident and get back to their daily lives.

Psalm 10:14 But Thou hast seen it, for Thou beholdest mischief and spite, to requite it with Thy hand. The poor committeth himself unto Thee; Thou art the helper of the fatherless.

The injustice and trauma to the survivor which is inherent to Inmate Partner Violence does not map with the way the current retributive justice system treats the survivor. Restorative justice practices, including Victim Offender Mediation, have the potential to benefit individual survivors of Inmate Partner Violence by providing answers, restored agency, and personal closure which can provide better and more holistic opportunities for healing and justice. Victim Offender Mediation can give survivors the ability to confront their particular concerns or questions, ranging from "What happened?" to "Why did this happen?" to "How can this be prevented in the future?" Survivors' experiences "are not monolithic and universal, but culturally diverse, highly contextual, and socially constructed." Each survivor will be the best source to determine how that survivor will best heal. Even so, many survivors find themselves exhibiting similar feelings and asking similar questions to one another. Receiving long-awaited answers to those questions directly from the offender can give survivors closure, understanding, and empowerment, allowing for holistic restoration for the survivor. Even being able to ask those questions grants survivors "opportunities to express and validate their emotions: their anger, their fear, their pain."

Victim Offender Mediation can benefit various types of victims. Those victims might include those who wish to maintain a positive relationship, even a romantic or intimate one, with their partner for various reasons. Such reasons might be emotional; love, cultural contexts, feeling that a great deal of effort has been put into a relationship, and even the time devoted to lengthier relationships might bolster a desire to save a relationship. Those reasons might also be practical. Practical factors that might lead a victim to continue an actively or formerly abusive intimate partner relationship may include bene-fits to children, property interests, housing opportunities, and lack of financial resources.

Encouraging accountability, restoring equality, and addressing future intentions in a controlled environment can encourage healthy reconciliation of certain relation- ships. Victim Offender Mediation can also benefit those survivors who wish to cut all ties to the abuser at the end of the process; restorative practices may give survivors the chance to heal independently of the relationship which predicated the abuse. Regardless of the survivor's future intentions regarding the offender, Victim Offender Mediation and other restorative practices can prepare survivors for continuing their lives normally by allowing holistic emotional, physical, relational, and financial healing.

Benefits to people who offend

An opportunity to make it right. People who offend have the opportunity to express remorse and apologize for their actions, benefiting themselves as well as their victims.

A way to put the incident behind them. People who offend have the opportunity to make significant and appropriate amends and then move on. They are able to return to their communities knowing that the matter is settled.

A timely resolution. The process of restorative justice is swift in comparison to the criminal justice system, so that offenders can more quickly make meaningful changes in their lives.

A high success rates. Restorative justice has a high rate of compliance or completion. Within a voluntary and non-coercive process, people who have offended tend to follow through on agreements that they have a part in creating.

Victim Offender Mediation has the potential to repair, reconcile, and reassure all parties to an offense within a society. First and foremost, restorative conferences like Victim Offender Mediation can benefit survivors of Inmate Partner Violence by increasing agency and lowering the risks of re-traumatization by continued court processes. Restorative conferences could also benefit the offenders themselves, improving their relationships, decreasing recidivism, and promoting successful reentry into society.

Finally, Victim Offender Mediation can benefit society, including families, communities, and the legal system, by restructuring the way society thinks about gender-based violence, best practices for healing and justice, and community and legal forgiveness. Holistic goals for justice can encourage a pervasive and structural change within society that could lower the rates of Inmate Partner Violence in the first place.

Offenders can benefit from restorative practices. Under traditional retributive justice models, offenders must "suffer for the suffering they have caused." Importantly, restorative justice theory views offenders holistically. Offenders are not defined by their offense; rather, they are viewed as entire people with the ability to improve for the betterment of those they have harmed, their communities, and themselves. Victim Offender Mediation can help offenders take responsibility for their actions, increase the offender's chance of successful reintegration into the community, and lower the chance they will perpetrate Inmate Partner Violence in the future.

Offenders, like survivors, might have the desire to continue the existing relationship in a healthy way for various emotional or practical factors. Offenders are, after all, one half of an intimate partner relationship, and they may weigh any of the same factors, such as love, children, housing, or finances. Offenders benefit by learning ways to participate healthily in future relationships with other intimate partners, thereby potentially forgoing future abusive cycles and reducing recidivism—a benefit to potential victims, the community, and themselves.

Benefits to the Community:

Reduced recidivism. Restorative justice has a high rate of success in reducing repeat offenses. When communities reintegrate their citizens after harm has been repaired, the likelihood of recidivism is greatly reduced. People who have offended have the opportunity to make things right, learn from the process, and put the matter behind them, so they can more easily go on to lead a crime-free life.

Increased safety. With reduced recidivism comes a safer community. Restorative justice empowers individuals to make their neighborhoods and towns safer and more pleasant places to live.

Cost effectiveness. A restorative approach to crime saves the state money by preventing individuals from becoming part of the criminal justice system for offenses that can be resolved at the local level with community and victim participation.

A stronger community. In addition to enhancing the safety and wellbeing of a town or region, community justice centers help to establish a more active citizenship. Volunteering has been shown to build stronger and more cohesive communities and increase the social networks within towns and neighborhoods.

Restructuring justice models to work better for survivors can help uproot the societal landscape that produces the history of violence against women in the first place, thus reducing rates of Inmate Partner Violence. Additionally, "Etching empathy into the restorative justice frame- work arms society with a capacity to understand and address what is broken in the lives of offenders, and it may even give credence to society's demand for accountability for the harm that has been inflicted." These restorative practices can be used before charges are filed in order to encourage accountability and healing while also minimizing the burden on courts.

Inmate Partner Violence damages the economy: the estimated costs of Inmate Partner Violence against women exceeded an estimated $5.8 billion in 2003. Those costs included direct costs of medical care, mental health care, lost productivity, and the value of lifetime earnings. Remnants of the power and control dynamic can have a lingering effect in the brain, leading to continued depression, anxiety, or isolation, which, aside from the inherent damage to the person, reduce work efficiency and skyrocket health costs.

Individuals who are not bound by un- resolved or unattended trauma may feel freer to contribute more to society, work harder, spend more freely, and feel less prone to isolation. Not only would lower rates of Inmate Partner Violence benefit individual survivors and offenders, but they would also improve the economy: the Center for Disease Control has stated that "until we reduce the incidence of Inmate Partner Violence in the United States, we will not reduce the eco- nomic and social burden of this problem." Holistic restorative jus- tice methods, including ones that integrate Victim Offender Mediation, could lessen the chance of revictimization, decreasing rates of Inmate Partner Violence and thereby boosting the economy.

Throughout the Bible, God seeks to strengthen families. Husbands are encouraged to love their wives, children to obey parents, and parents to train up their children in the right paths. The Bible contains many real-life examples of both happy and divided families. In the same token, society has an interest in keeping families together. Short-term and long-term, children benefit financially, emotion- ally, and educationally from having two parents. Specifically, children benefit from having two parents in a healthy relationship, even if coparenting and not in a romantic relationship. Children benefit less from coparenting when there is a history of violence.

However, long-term coparenting outcomes depend on the type of Inmate Partner Violence. Couples who experience coercive controlling violence, which is rooted in continuous control and involves monitoring, isolating, and inciting fear in the victim, may experience less successful coparenting after separation due to a perceived "threat to an abuser's control over his partner and children." Conversely, couples who experience situational couple violence, which is the result of specific situations "without a relationship-wide motive to coercively control a partner" may experience healthier and more successful coparenting due to a bilateral perception of a more equal relationship. Restorative justice offers positive reconciliation for diverse relationships, even involving children, because it prioritizes safety and relationships on equal grounds.

Three themes, common to both offenders and victims are:

a): Most offenders as a child, were physically abused.

b): As an adult, are psychologically and spiritually abused, which wounded their sense of themself and their relationship to the world.

Wherefore, for genuine healing to take place there are two preconditions that need to be met.:

a): repentance

b): and forgiveness.

For criminals to be set free, they must repent and be converted - turn around and have a change of heart. They must humble themselves, seek God's face, and turn from their evil ways.

The victim can find peace, no matter what the offender chooses to do - or not do. The victim's ability to forgive must not be contingent upon the repentance of the criminal. Victims can choose for themselves - life or death: a life of peace and love with forgiveness - or a life of hatred, anger and bitterness with unforgiveness.

Often people mistakenly think that forgiveness means:

a): forgetting what happened,

b): writing it off,

c): or perhaps letting the victimizer off the hook easily.

But forgiveness actually means:

a): Forgiveness is letting go of the power the offense and the offender have over a person.

b): It means no longer letting that offense and offender dominate.

Just putting it behind you. The word "forgive" means to wipe the slate clean, to pardon, to cancel a debt. It is important to remember that forgiveness is not granted because a person deserves to be forgiven. Instead, it is an act of love, mercy, and grace.

Without this experience of forgiveness, without this closure:

a): the wounds may fester

b): the violation may take over our consciousness and our lives.

c): The offense and the offender are in control.

But all this will change when we forgive. It doesn't mean we will put ourselves back into a harmful situation or that we suddenly accept or approve of the person's criminal behavior. It simply means we set down our anger and bitterness regarding the crime they committed against us. We forgive them because God forgave us (Ephesians 4:31-32 and Romans 5:8).

Real forgiveness, then, is an act of empowerment and healing that allows a person to move from victim to survivor.

What are some of the conditions that help forgiveness to happen?

a): An expression of responsibility,

b): regret,

c): repentance on the part of an offender can be a powerful help.

Americans have fallen into a dangerous trend. We are lawsuit happy. We sue for everything from a hot cup of coffee to hurt feelings. Forgiveness has become a lost art. Now everything is about revenge, getting even, making someone pay. What directives are given to us by God regarding forgiveness in the following verses?

a) Matthew 6:12: And forgive us our debts, as we forgive our debtors.

When most people get to this verse, they tend to ignore the second half. We are asking God to forgive us our sins, but in effect, we are asking God to use the same measure of forgiveness for us as we have given to others. When we take this verse to heart, we should be fearful to hold grudges against others.

b) Ephesians 4:31-32: 31 Let all bitterness, wrath, anger, clamor, and evil speaking be put away from you, with all malice. 32 And be kind to one another, tenderhearted, forgiving one another, even as God in Christ forgave you.

It is impossible to spend any amount of time with someone and not be offended about something. When someone has offended us, we should forgive him, even if s/he does not ask us to.

c) Mark 11:25: And whenever you stand praying, if you have anything against anyone, forgive him, that your Father in heaven may also forgive you your trespasses.

d) 1 Corinthians 13:5: does not behave rudely, does not seek its own, is not provoked, thinks no evil;

An unforgiving person might goad another, or speak rudely to them, but the loving person should not lash out or seek revenge.

e) 1 Peter 4:8: And above all things have fervent love for one another, for "love will cover a multitude of sins."

In our relationships with one another, love is the most important thing. The word for "fervent" or "deeply" here comes from a word describing how an athlete strains and stretches his muscles to win a race. This kind of deliberate and determined love allows us to overlook the imperfections and sins that everyone has. This kind of love points people to God, who will, out of love and through His grace, forgive all their sins when they put their faith in Him.

f) Galatians 6:1: Brethren, if a man is overtaken in any trespass, you who are spiritual restore such a one in a spirit of gentleness, considering yourself lest you also be tempted.

In the Christian community, everyone's spiritual life is everyone's business. The purpose is not to be nosey or to cause trouble, but rather to help each other work towards the goal of perfection. If someone is caught sinning, we should forgive him and help him get back on the right track.

g) 2 Corinthians 2:7: so that, on the contrary, you ought rather to forgive and comfort him, lest perhaps such a one be swallowed up with too much sorrow.

A definition for forgiveness could be giving up my right or desire to hurt you, for hurting me.

How many times did Peter think would be the proper number of times to forgive a brother? (Matthew 18:21): Up to seven times

Though there is no limit placed on forgiveness in the Old Testament, the rabbis of Jesus' time often taught that it was proper to forgive an offence no more than three times. Peter thought he was being extra generous by offering to forgive people seven times. Jesus exposes such legalistic limitations for what they are.

Peter had a definite rationale for asking if we should forgive that many times. The Jews had ruled that one could only be forgiven three times, but never a fourth. Knowing that Jesus would show more mercy than the Jews, he must have thought seven times was more than fair.

Jesus put a strong emphasis on forgiveness. How many times did He tell Peter we should forgive a transgressor? (Matthew18:22): Seventy times seven.

When Jesus suggested that we should forgive 490 times, He did not mean that we should keep a list, and cut off forgiveness when a person offends us the 491st time. He was trying to show the absurdity of "forgiving" someone a certain number of times. Such list keeping reveals a begrudging spirit, rather than a forgiving one.

This is the kind of forgiving attitude that God shows us. Christians are not perfect, and most of us commit some sins every day. When we confess these sins, God forgives us. Part of repentance is making an effort not to repeat sins, but we continue to do some sins out of either habit or carelessness. Even still, God continuously forgives us. This does not diminish the seriousness of sin, but it does show how merciful God is.

Forgiveness is both a choice and a mandate.

According to Matthew 6:14, what is the Lord's design for forgiveness? For if you forgive men their trespasses, your heavenly Father will also forgive you.

What is the result of an unforgiving spirit? (Matthew 6:15): But if you do not forgive men their trespasses, neither will your Father forgive your trespasses.

This is the spiritual application of the Golden Rule: do unto others and you would have them do unto you (Luke 6:31). God is very willing to forgive us, and we likewise should forgive others. When we are in a close relationship with God, this forgiving attitude becomes natural, especially when we realize how much we have been forgiven (Luke 7:36-50). Those who do not know God will have little, if any, capability to forgive. Forgiveness is a sign that a person knows about true love from God. A grudging heart is a symptom of one's lack of relationship with God.

Forgiveness will set: both the offender and the offended person free.

Forgiveness is a life-long process.

Recently, a survey was made of 200 married adults with regard to forgiveness, and not only forgiveness of their spouse but also of others. The researchers were wondering how a person's ability to forgive others would affect their marital satisfaction and personal well-being.

The results were astounding! This research found that there is a huge relationship between satisfaction in the marriage and forgiveness. As a matter of fact, they concluded that as much as one third of happiness in the marriage was related to forgiveness. Not only did they find the ability to forgive impacted the relationship between the spouses, they found it was significantly related to personal emotional problems. As the ability to forgive went up, individuals reported fewer symptoms of depression, anxiety, and fatigue.

These results suggest that all counselors, both secular and faith-based, should spend time helping people develop a forgiving attitude.

The church has not successfully fulfilled their critical responsibility in helping people navigate the process of forgiveness.

Incarcerated believers who make up the "church-behind-the-walls" have the same needs as believers in the "outside world" for instruction, for living by example, and for being equipped to do ministry. Local churches play an important role not only in sharing the gospel with incarcerated non-believers, but also in supporting, teaching and equipping saints in the incarcerated church for ministry in their environment. Sadly, this need is not being fully met.

Contrary to popular belief, offenders often do feel guilt for what they have done. This sense of guilt results in offenders becoming consumed by tremendous fears.

What is one of their greatest fears?
Zero state. that is, personal worthlessness.

This is a feeling of being inferior to others in some way. It is often unconscious, and frequently drives people to overcompensate, resulting either in spectacular achievement or extreme antisocial behavior. Most of us have struggled with such feeling from time to time. For some, it's just an occasional problem. But for others, it's a pervasive problem that cripples them emotionally, making it impossible to successfully reach their goals.

These are people who are convinced that whatever they do will eventually result in failure. They often avoid starting up a new task because they are sure it will be a vain effort. Even when they succeed, they are easily frustrated and are ready to quit for the slightest reasons. They are easily put off when any obstacles get in their way. They are easily discouraged by criticisms from others and tend to lose confidence in themselves, God, or their organization when accusations are hurled.

Such zero-state thinking and attitudes keep us from fulfilling God's plan for our lives. But this is nothing new to God. He's been dealing with man's feelings of inadequacy since Old Testament times. When we ask, the Spirit of God will make us competent to do everything God asks us to do, with the help of Christ who gives us the strength, power and ability.

What are some defensive techniques many criminals adopt to avoid feeling guilty, and to maintain their sense of self-worth?

a): "exculpatory strategies" to deflect or deny their guilt.

b): They may argue, for example, that everyone does it, that the victim deserved or could afford the losses, or that they were provoked beyond reason.

c): They may adopt the language of the social and psychological determinism, arguing that "I'm depraved because I'm deprived."

d): Themselves, some offenders even develop elaborate fantasies about who they are and what they did.

In addition, offenders with the zero-state thinking error often believe that God cannot use them. They may think:

• I have no talents that God can use.

• I have no gifts.
• I have no ability.
• I have no education.
• I have no experience.
• I have no opportunity.

But by God's grace, He can use all of us for Kingdom work - no matter who we are, no matter what we've done, no matter what skills or talents we think we lack. God is just waiting for us to make ourselves available.

When the debt has been paid in full to society, a criminal's guilt does not end. New life requires both forgiveness and confession. For offenders to be truly whole, they must a): confess wrongdoing, b): admitting their responsibility c): acknowledging the harm done.

Repentance, confession, and forgiveness by God or by the victim does not eliminates the consequences of the offender's actions.

The criminal justice system discourages the processes of reconciliation. The legal process itself has no real place for repentance, and certainly not for forgiveness. Moreover, by its nature, it encourages offenders to deny their guilt and to focus on their own situations.

In Acts 7, we see a Biblical example of how victims should respond to acts violence of themselves. As he was being stoned to death, Stephen refused to harbor an unforgiving spirit against his executioners. What compelled the Jews to stone Stephen? (Acts 7:55-57): When he said: I see the heavens opened and the Son of Man standing at the right hand of God!"

When Stephen declared that he saw Jesus standing at the right hand of God, it was too much. That was the final straw. The Sanhedrin reacted quickly, violently, and united. Remember when Jesus, standing before this same body of men, declared that He would sit at the right hand of God, they had the same reaction and sealed his death as a blasphemer (Matthew 26:64-66).

Saul watched over the garments of the witnesses as they stoned Stephen. (Acts 7:58)

Saul was deeply involved in this whole process and became the official overseer of the incident. It may even be that he was the one who had stirred up the mob into a frenzy.

a) Did Stephen pray for those who were stoning him or curse them? He prayed for them.

b) What was Stephen's final prayer as he died? (vs. 60): Lord, do not charge them with this sin.

If anybody ever had good reason to be angry and bitter, Stephen did. The rage of others was literally killing him, but he did not rage. Instead, he prayed: "Lord, do not hold this sin against them." Even in this violent and painful death, Stephen recognized that God could forgive the executioners. He did not ask for revenge. His final gracious prayer was that these violent and ungodly people would be saved.

How could Stephen be so forgiving, even as he was also being the victim? (Thought question - answers will vary): Stephen was full of the Holy Spirit. And one of the gifts of the Spirit is to love or enemies

Stephen could not do it under his own power. In death, the tranquil faith of Stephen as he was stoned stood in sharp contrast to the others' brutal and lethal anger. And by his own testimony, it was a contrast that haunted Saul afterwards.

From Stephen's example, we learn that forgiveness must be Unconditional, Genuine and sincere, For everyone, regardless of the offense, and even until death.

Unforgiveness makes a good death impossible. Forgiveness can make an ugly death beautiful.

The time of death is not the place to learn the art of forgiveness. When the muscles of forgiveness are weak from disuse in life, the time of death can unleash a font of bitterness. I have seen this personally. On the other hand, if the art of forgiveness has been well-practiced in life, then the threshold of death offers no obstacle to forgiveness and no platform for bitterness. Stephen faced death with no bitterness in his heart, with a readiness to forgive, because, by the power and grace of God, he practiced the art of forgiveness throughout his life.

Apostle Paul was the person present at Stephen's execution, who later changed his ways and served the Lord faithfully for the rest of his life, in contrast, Jesus displayed this same forgiving spirit, even as he was being put to death? (Luke 23:34).

Stephen so modeled Jesus in his manner of dying that even his last sentences were similar to those spoken by Jesus on the cross (Luke 23:46).

Why is it so degrading to be a victim?

Denial of victims' autonomy by offenders is in large part what makes being a victim so traumatic. Offenders turn victims into objects, into things, robbing them of power over their own lives. This is deeply degrading.

Not only that, if the person responsible for the crime can be identified, the criminal justice system, which can be bewildering, becomes involved. Victims can be left feeling that they have totally lost complete control over their lives and what is happening to them.

Some of the ways by which victims attempt to reassert their sense of autonomy are:

a): Some, it is regained simply by overcoming, by living successfully, by becoming survivors.

b): For some, it is done by taking safeguards or otherwise finding ways to make their lives their own again.

c): Some attempt to meet it by demands for revenge and punishment.

d): Some are able to find empowerment through an act of Christian forgiveness.

All crimes to greater or lesser degree qualify as traumatic events. All threaten or take away a person's or family's sense of safety, security, control and predictability. Yet, often the victims try to minimize the effects, act brave, get on with their lives, and rationalize that the effect wasn't as bad as it could have been. However, all the ways listed above help the victim move beyond that stage.

Furthermore, one of the ways by which offenders attempt to reassert their sense of autonomy is by finding another victim to dominate.

There are probably more men than women raped in the United States every year - most of them in prison. Best estimates put the annual number of prison rapes at about 140,000, which is 50,000 more than the 90,000 or so rapes of women reported to police. Gang rape of the most brutal kind is common, and weaker prisoners often seek protection from a "daddy" who fights off other predators in exchange for total submission and sex on demand.

In addition, there is an ugly racial dimension to prison rape. Blacks and Mexicans deliberately seek out white victims, and black-on-white rape is probably more common than any other kind. Prison rape is an appalling secret in a country that prides itself on human rights. Suicide is the leading cause of death in prisons, and is the only way out for some rape victims.

Many poor people believe that they don't have choices or real power to determine their destinies. Instead, if they are successful or arrested for a crime, they believe it is due to good or bad luck.

From an earthly perspective, things may seem to happen at random, resulting in good or bad luck for a person. But throughout the whole of Scripture, it is clear that God is in control of all of His creation. He is fully able to take acts of natural law, the free will of both good and evil men, and the wicked intent of demons - and combine them all to accomplish His good and perfect will.   For any event of life, no matter how small (Matthew 10:29-31) or how large (Daniel 4:35; Proverbs 21:1), God is sovereign over all (Ephesians 1:11; Psalm 115:3; Isaiah 46:9-10). Nothing is simply a matter of luck.

Many people in our society lack a sense of personal power and crime can be a way of asserting such power, but this doesn't work. Personal power comes from embracing spiritual values rather than earthly values. It comes from loving the Lord and living for Him, making love, kindness and compassion more important than power over others.

The entire judicial system is designed to rob offenders of their personal sense of autonomy. Hereto are the few of the ways by which they accomplish this:

a): They are treated as pawns in the process.

b): They are sent to prison,

c): They are further deprived of a sense of power and worth unless they can derive some from the warped subculture of prison.

You would think that the purpose of controls in prison would be for social purposes - peaceful co-existence among the inmates and rehabilitation. But the truth is, the controls are in place for the sake of crushing individuality and personal freedom. Prison buildings become spaces where state agents are dedicated to maintaining state power, exacting revenge and enforcing discipline on those who fail to abide by system rules.

Judge Challeen has noted that many offenders who appear before him are, by society's standards, losers. People who see themselves as such are more likely than others to assert their identities through crime and less likely to be deterred by the fear of consequences.

Society today tags people as losers if they are unattractive, poor, slower to learn, live on the wrong side of town, or drive a beat-up car. Surprisingly, even nerds who are quite intelligent are often considered to be losers by the "in" crowd. But God sees people as losers if they are disobedient, greedy, prideful, self-absorbed or doubters. In Bible times, many saw the Jews as losers - and yet they were the people closest to God's heart. He even sent His Son to save mankind through the Jewish race.

Working class children tend to see their defeats not as losers, but rather as victims.

What are some of the reasons that "crime" has become prominent in media coverage?

a): Studies have found that it is so in part because it sells.

b): People are drawn to the sensational.

c): coverage is prominent also because it is "easy news."

Crimes easily snag the top headline, and each time the news comes back on, listeners hang on every word to see if one more detail is revealed. Following are possible reasons for this.

Readers or listeners often want an explanation of why crimes happen. They ask: "Could it happen to me?" They may want to know so that they can prevent a similar thing happening to themselves.

Your readers and listeners need to know how laws are broken, and how people who break laws are caught and punished. This helps them understand what laws are and what are the penalties for breaking them.

Most people obey the law, so crime stories are about unusual events - one of the criteria for news.

Some people are interested in the way criminals get something without much effort. For example, although a gang of crooks may spend weeks or months planning a robbery to net them $100,000, it might take ordinary workers many years of effort to earn that much legally. Some crimes may fascinate people who obey the laws but who wonder what it might be like to break them.

Criminals take risks and face punishment if they are caught. This may make them fascinating to read or hear about.

Crime news is often accepted by reporters from official sources without question and without independent verification.

What are two results of crime news being obtained and viewed through the eyes of the legal process and its professionals?

To be abstracted and mystified.

How is crime used as an important tool by politicians? Crime can be an important beating stick.

What are two ways a community can respond to crime?

a): We can draw together defensively, against the "enemy." A sense of community may be increased, but it is a defensive, exclusive, threatened community.

b): Alternately, we can retire to fortified homes, becoming distrustful of others.

It is true that the issue of how we respond to wrongdoing has important implications for our future and the future of our nation. Why people do commit crimes so readily today?

One of the reasons it is because of the way the judicial system responds to criminal acts.

a) How does Ecclesiastes 8:11 tell us we should respond to wrongdoing?

Because the sentence against an evil work is not executed speedily. Actually, this is not only advice from God - it is also listed as a right of the offender in the 6th Amendment. "In all criminal prosecutions, the accused shall enjoy the right to a speedy and public trial, by an impartial jury of the State and district wherein the crime shall have been committed, which district shall have been previously ascertained by law, and to be informed of the nature and cause of the accusation; to be confronted with the witnesses against him; to have compulsory process for obtaining witnesses in his favor, and to have the Assistance of Counsel for his defense."

b) What does this verse predict will happen if crime is not handled in this manner?

The heart of the sons of men is fully set in them to do evil. Would you agree that this is certainly an issue in the U.S. today?

Often life seems unfair, many good people suffer, many wicked people prosper. Often the forces of evil seem stronger than the forces of good. People seem to get by with evil. But it's the final score that counts. God knows what has happened, and He will take care of it Summary: Benefits of restorative justice.

Restorative justice practices have several benefits, including:

1. Healing for Victims: Restorative justice practices focus on addressing the needs and concerns of victims, providing them with a voice and an opportunity to express how they have been impacted by the harm. This can provide healing and closure for victims, and help them move forward from the experience.

2. Accountability for Offenders: Restorative justice practices also focus on holding offenders accountable for their actions in a way that is meaningful and restorative. This can help offenders understand the impact of their behavior on others, take responsibility for their actions, and work to make amends.

3. Community Building: Restorative justice practices promote community building and collaboration, bringing together victims, offenders, and community members to work towards healing and restoration. This can help build stronger and more supportive communities, and promote a sense of social cohesion and shared responsibility.
4. Reduced Recidivism: Restorative justice practices have been shown to be effective in reducing recidivism rates, as offenders who participate in restorative justice programs are more likely to take responsibility for their actions and work towards making positive changes in their lives.
5. Cost-Effective: Restorative justice practices can be more cost-effective than traditional criminal justice approaches, as they can reduce the burden on the criminal justice system and promote more positive outcomes for victims and offenders.
6. Empowerment of Participants: Restorative justice practices empower participants by giving them a voice and a role in the process, and by promoting personal accountability and responsibility. This can lead to greater feelings of empowerment, self-efficacy, and personal growth.

Accordingly, restorative justice practices offer a more holistic and inclusive approach to justice that can promote healing, accountability, and community building, while also reducing recidivism rates and promoting more cost-effective outcomes.

CHAPTER V
RETRIBUTIVE JUSTICE

Retributive Justice

Retributive justice is a system of criminal justice that focuses solely on punishment of law breakers and the compensation of victims, in contrast, the deterrence—prevention of future crimes—or the rehabilitation of offenders. In general, retributive justice is based on the principle that the severity of the punishment should be in proportion to the seriousness of the crime committed.

Retribution is simultaneously with restorative principles in law codes from the ancient Near East, including the Code of Ur-Nammu (c. 2050 BC) [The Code of Ur-Nammu is the oldest known law code surviving today. It is from Mesopotamia and is written on tablets, in the Sumerian language c. 2100–2050 BC], the Laws of Eshnunna (c. 2000 BC) [The Laws of Eshnunna (abrv. LE) are inscribed on two cuneiform tablets discovered in Tell Abū Harmal, Baghdad, Iraq. The Iraqi Directorate of Antiquities headed by Taha Baqir unearthed two parallel sets of tablets in 1945 and 1947. The two tablets are separate copies of an older source and date back to ca. 1930 BC], and the better-known Babylonian Code of Hammurabi (c. 1750 BC) [The Code of Hammurabi is a Babylonian legal text composed c. 1755–1750 BC. It is the longest, best-organized, and best-preserved legal text from the ancient Near East. It is written in the Old Babylonian dialect of Akkadian, purportedly by Hammurabi, sixth king of the First Dynasty of Babylon]. In those legal systems, collectively referred to as cuneiform law, crimes were considered violations of other people's rights. Victims were to be compensated for the intentional and unintentional harms they suffered, and offenders were to be punished because they had done wrong.

Retribution is based on the concept of the law of retaliation known as lex talionis. At its core is the principle of equal and direct retribution, as impeccably exhibited in [Exodus 21:24 eye for eye, tooth for tooth, hand for hand, foot for foot,] as "an eye for an eye." Destroying the tooth of a person of equal social standing meant that one's own tooth would be removed, inter-alia, destroying the eye of a person of equal social standing meant that one's own eye would be put out, to wit. Some penalties designed to punish culpable behavior by individuals were specifically tied to outlawed acts. Branders who used their skills to remove slave marks from runaway slaves, for example, had their hands amputated.

While an abstract idea of retribution dates way back to pre-biblical times, consequently, retributive justice has played a major role in current thinking about the punishment of lawbreakers, the ultimate justification for it remains contested and problematic.

Theory and Principles of Retributive Justice

Retributive justice is founded on the theorem that when an individual commits a crime, "justice" requires that he/she be punished in return and that the severity of his/her punishment should be proportionate to the solemnity of their crime.

While the idea, theorem, method, or the concept has been used in a variety of ways, retributive justice is best recognized as that form of justice committed to the following three principles:

- Those who commit crimes–especially serious crimes—morally deserve to suffer a proportionate punishment.
- The punishment should be determined and applied by officials of a legitimate criminal justice system.
- It is morally impermissible to intentionally punish the innocent or to inflict disproportionately harsh punishments on wrongdoers.

Disengaging it from sheer revenge, retributive justice should not be personal. In contrast, it is administered only at the wrongdoing involved, has inherent limits, seeks no pleasure from the suffering of wrongdoers, and employs clearly defined procedural standards.

Pursuant to the fundamental's truth, propositions and practices of procedural and substantive law the government through prosecution before a judge must establish the guilt of a person for violation of the law. Following the determination of guilt, a judge imposes the appropriate sentence, which can include a fine, probation, imprisonment, and in extreme cases, the death penalty.

Consequently, retributive justice is to be executed swiftly and must cost the lawbreaker something, which does not include the collateral consequences of the crime, such as the pain of emotional trauma and suffering of the malefactor's family.

Retribution of offenders also serves to restore balance to community or society by gratifying the public's desire for vengeance. The transgressors are considered to have misused society's benefits and have thus gained an unethical advantage over their law-abiding counterparts. Retributive which is contrast to restorative punishment, removes that advantage and tries to restore balance to society by validating how individuals ought to behave in society. Punishing wrongdoers for their crimes also reminds others in the public that such conduct is inappropriate for law-abiding citizens, thus helping to deter further wrongdoing.

Historic Context

The concept and theorem of retribution appears in the ancient codes of laws from the ancient Near East, including the Babylonian Code of Hammurabi from around 1750 BCE. In this and other ancient legal systems, collectively referred to as cuneiform law, crimes were considered to have violated other people's rights. Victims were to be compensated for the intentional and unintentional harms they suffered, and offenders were to be punished because they had done wrong.

King Hammurabi was an important Babylonian king known best for an early law code, that we refer to by his name. He united Mesopotamia and turned Babylonia into an important power.

Some refer to Hammurabi as Hammurapi

Code of Hammurabi

Hammurabi is now synonymous with his code of laws, referred to as the Code of Hammurabi. Five columns of the stele on which his laws were written (inscribed) have been erased. Scholars estimate the total number of legal judgments contained on the stele when it was intact would have been around 300.

The stele may not actually contain laws, per se, as judgments made by Hammurabi. By recording the judgments, he made, the stele would have served to testify to and honor King Hammurabi's acts and deeds.

Hammurabi and the Bible

Hammurabi may have been the Biblical Amraphel, King of Sennaar, mentioned in the Bible book of Genesis.

Hammurabi Dates

Hammurabi was the sixth king of the First Babylonian dynasty -- about 4000 years ago. We don't know for sure when -- during a general period running from 2342 to 1050 B.C. -- he ruled, but the standard Middle Chronology puts his dates at 1792-1750. (Put that date in context by looking at the major events timeline.) [Source] King Hammurabi of Babylonia - Biographical Profile (thoughtco.com)

As a philosophy of justice, retribution recurs in many religious sects. There are mentions of it in several religious texts, including the

Infallible Word, Bible. Adam and Eve, for example, were cast out of the Garden of Eden because they violated God's rules of not eating fruit of knowledge of good and evil, and thus deserved to be punished. In the Pentateuch, the Torahic law, Exodus 21:24 direct retribution is expressed as "an eye for an eye, "an eye for an eye, a tooth for a tooth." Plucking out the eye of a person of equal social standing meant that one's own eye would be put out. Some penalties designed to punish culpable behavior by individuals were specifically tied to outlawed acts. Thieves, for example, had their hands amputated.

The German philosopher and Central Enlightenment thinker Immanuel Kant, in the 18th century developed a theory of retribution based on logic and reason. In Kant's observations and reckoning, the only purpose punishment should serve is to penalize the lawbreakers for committing a crime. To Kant, the punishment's effect on the criminal's likelihood of being rehabilitated is irrelevant, which is the main purpose of restorative justice, "restoration". The punishment is there to punish the lawbreakers for the crime they have committed—nothing more, nothing less. Kant's theories created, coupled with the very nature of retributive justice fueled the arguments of Kant's modern critics who argue that his approach would lead to harsh and ineffective sentencing. The Gospel of Matthew quotes Isaiah 7:14: "'The virgin will be with child and will give birth to a son, and they will call him Immanuel'—which means, 'God with us'" (Matthew 1:23 NIV). Although philosopher Immanuel Kant (1724–1804) bore the name meaning "God with us," his ideas resulted in skepticism that places God beyond us.

Kant's views led to the theory of "just deserts," or the now more prominent views on the subject of the punishment of criminals that offenders must deserve to be punished. Ask people on the street why criminals should be punished, and most of them are likely to say "because they 'deserve' it."

Being discerning of philosophy requires some level of familiarity and understanding of it. Moreover, not all philosophy is "bad". "Good philosophy must exist, if for no other reason, because bad philosophy needs to be answered." Learning to interact with, and respond intelligently to, philosophical ideas is part of the Christian calling to love God with all of our minds and to defend the faith (see Matthew 22:37 Jesus replied: "'Love the Lord your God with all your heart and with all your soul and with all your mind and 1 Peter 3:15 But in your hearts revere Christ as Lord. Always be prepared to give an answer to everyone who asks you to give the reason for the hope that you have. But do this with gentleness and respect).

Philosophy is the "love of wisdom." Wisdom includes the ability to make correct judgments based on a proper understanding of reality. Any thoughtful study of philosophy requires familiarity with the basic terms of the discipline. Three questions summarize main areas of philosophical study: (1) What is ultimate reality? (2) How do we know? and (3) How should this knowledge of ultimate reality guide our conduct?

Philosopher Kant goes on to suggest that adhering to the law is a sacrifice of one's right to freedom of choice. Therefore, those that break the laws gain an unfair advantage over those that do not. Punishment, therefore, is necessary as a means to rectify the balance between the law-abiding citizens and the criminals, removing any unfairly gained advantage from the criminals.

Many legal scholars argue that widespread adoption of Kant's theories has resulted in a trend of modern criminal justice systems to criminalize too much conduct, such as the simple possession of small amounts of marijuana, and to punish those conducts too severely—or to "over-prosecute" and "over-sentence."

Today, unification of the current system of retributive justice, with a recently developed approach of restorative justice has shown promise in reducing the harshness of contemporary sentencing while also providing meaningful relief to crime victims. Restorative justice seeks to evaluate the harmful impact of a crime on its victims and determine what can be done to best repair that harm while holding the person or persons who caused it accountable for their actions. Through organized face-to-face meetings among all parties connected to a crime, the goal of restorative justice is to reach an agreement on what the offender can do to repair the harm caused by their offense rather than simply handing out punishment. Critics of such an approach argue that it can create conflicts between the reconciliation objective of restorative justice and the condemnatory objective of retributive punishment.

Prisons were originally promoted as a humane alternative to corporal and capital punishment.

For most of history, imprisoning was not a punishment in itself, but rather a way to confine criminals until corporal or capital punishment was administered. Only in the 19th century, beginning in Britain, did prisons as known today become commonplace.

There are two types of people in jail or prison: those who were wrongfully accused and victimized by an unjust system, and those who are guilty and whose punishment is just according to the system of law they have broken. The Bible has something to say to both the innocent and guilty who are in jail/prison. To the guilty, the Bible recommends truth and submission to the laws of the government, and it offers freedom from the spiritual prison of sin—freedom that comes through the person of Christ – Romans 6:18. To the innocent and wrongfully accused, the Bible offers peace, patience, and hope in difficult circumstances, as well as the hope of heavenly reward.

Pursuant to Encyclopedias – International Standard Bible Encyclopedia, Prison or prisoner is priz'-n, priz'-'-n-er, priz'-ner (there are various Hebrew words which are rendered "prison" in the King James Version, among them:

1. Hebrew Words:

(1) cohar, "round house," "fortress" (8 times in Genesis), (2) kele' "restraint," "confinement" (12 times: in historic books, Isaiah, Jeremiah, with "house"), (3) maTTarah, "guard," "sentry" (13 times in Jeremiah and Nehemiah), (4) mahaphekheth, "distorting," i.e., stocks or pillory (4 times), (5) 'ecur, "bond," "fetters" Ecclesiastes 4:14 and Jeremiah 37:15); "ward" in the King James Version is usually the rendering for mishmar):

2. In Early Times:

The earliest occurrence of the word "prison" in the King James Version is found in the narrative of Joseph's life in Egypt (the Jahwist). The term used, namely, cohar, means perhaps "round house" or "tower." It seems probable that among the Hebrews there were no special buildings erected as "jails" in the premonarchical period, and perhaps not before the post-exilic period, when the adoption of the civic institutions and customs of surrounding nations prevailed. In Egypt and Assyria, on the contrary, there were probably public buildings corresponding to our modern jails. Among the Hebrews, rooms in connection with the royal palace or the residence of prominent court officials would be used for the purpose.

3. Joseph in Egypt:

According to one narrative (Jahwist) in Genesis the prison in which Joseph was confined had a "keeper," while according to another narrative (the Elohist) the offending members of the royal household, namely, the royal butler and the royal baker, were placed "in ward" with the "captain of the guard" in charge, i.e., in some part of the royal palace. This is still more probable if, instead of "captain of the guard," we should translate "chief of the cooks" i.e., superintendent of the royal kitchen.

4. Causes of Imprisonment:

It was often necessary to restrict the liberty of individuals who for various causes were a menace to those in authority, without inflicting any corporal punishment, e.g. Joseph's brethren were kept "in ward" three days - Genesis 42:19; Shimei was forbidden to pass beyond the boundary of Jerusalem - 1 Kings 2:36; the person who was caught gathering sticks on the Sabbath was put "in ward" pending his trial - Numbers 15:34. In the monarchical period, prophets who criticized the throne were put in prison, e.g. Micaiah by Ahab – 1 Kings 22:27, Hanani by Asa – 2 Chronicles 16:10. Hoshea, after his abortive effort to institute an alliance with So or Seve, king of Egypt, was shut up in prison by Shalmaneser - 2 Kings 17:4; compare also – 2 Kings 25:27 (Jehoiachin in Babylon); - Jeremiah 52:11 (Zedekiah in Babylon).

5. Under the Monarchy:

The Book of Jeremiah throws considerable light on the prison system of Jerusalem in the later monarchical period. The prophet was put "in the stocks that were in the upper gate of Benjamin, which was in the house of Yahweh" (20:2). Mere imprisonment was not adequate punishment for the prophet's announcement of Judah's doom; it was necessary to have recourse to the pillory. During the siege of Jerusalem Jeremiah was confined in the "court of the guard, which was in the king of Judah's house" (32:2, etc.). The "court of the guard" was evidently the quarters of the sentry who guarded the royal palace. According to the narrative of Jeremiah 37, the prophet was arrested on a charge of treachery and put in prison "in the house of Jonathan the scribe" (37:15). This verse does not necessarily mean that a private house was used as a prison. The words are capable of another interpretation, namely, that a building known as the "house of Jonathan the scribe" had been taken over by the authorities and converted into a jail. We read in the following verse that the house had a "dungeon" (literally, "house of the pit") and "cabins" or "cells."

6. The Treatment of Prisoners:

The data are not sufficient to enable us to give any detailed description of the treatment of prisoners. This treatment varied according to the character of the offense which led to incarceration. Samson during the period of his imprisonment was compelled to do hard labor Judges 16:21. Grinding was the occupation of women, and marked the depth of Samson's humiliation. Dangerous persons were subjected to various kinds of physical mutilation, e.g., Samson was deprived of his sight. This was a common practice in Assyria - 2 Kings 25:7. The thumbs and great toes of Adonibezek were cut off to render him incapable of further resistance Judges 1:6.

Various forms of torture were in vogue. Hanani the seer was put into the pillory by Asa (for "in a prison house" we should render "in the stocks"; see the Revised Version margin). In Jeremiah 29:26 for "prison," we should render "stocks" (so the Revised Version (British and American)) or "pillory," and for "stocks," "collar" (as in the Revised Version margin). the King James Version renders a different Hebrew word by "stocks" in Job (13:27; 33:11). There was a special prison diet 1 Kings 22:27, as well as a prison garb 2 Kings 25:29.

7. Other Hebrew Words:

There are other Hebrew words rendered "prison" (sometimes incorrectly) in the King James Version. In Psalms 142:7, the word which is translated as "prison" means a "place of execution," and is derived from a root that denotes, for instance, the isolation of the leper Leviticus 13:5; compare 24:22; 42:7). In Isaiah 53:8 "oppression" not "prison" is the correct translation while in Isaiah 61:1 the Hebrew denotes "opening of the eyes," rather than "opening of the prison." Prisoners are promised "light after darkness, gleam after gloom."

8. In the New Testament:

In the New Testament "prison" generally occurs for the Greek word phulake, which corresponds to the Hebrew word mishmar, referred to above (Matthews 5:25; Mark 6:17; Luke 3:20; Acts 5:19; 1 Peter 3:19), the King James Version renders this word by two different words, namely, "hold" and "cage"; the Revised Version (British and American) employs "hold" in each case (the Revised Version margin "prison"). In one passage "ward" is the rendering in the King James Version - Acts 12:10. In connection with the imprisonment of John the term used is desmoterion, "place of bonds" or "fetters" – Matthew 11:2; the same word is used in the case of Peter and John – Acts 5:21,23, and of Paul and Silas – Acts 16:26. But the more common term is also found in these narratives. In Acts 12:17 "prison" renders a Greek word which means "dwelling." In Acts 5:18 the King James Version, "prison" is the rendering for another Greek word, namely, teresis, "watching" or "ward" (the Revised Version (British and American) "ward"). In Acts 4:3, the King James Version employs "hold" as the rendering for the same word. This would correspond to the modern "police station" or "lockup."

Prison "alternatives" have expanded, and the "net" of control and intervention has widened

a) but without discernible effects on crime and

b) and without meeting essential needs of victim or offender.

Because the state and federal governments set standards for sentencing, there is no uniformity from courtroom to courtroom, and from judge to judge, in handing down sentences for the same crime.

When we identify something as a crime, a number of basic assumptions shape our responses.

What do we assume?

a): Guilt must be assigned.

b): The guilty must get their "just deserts."

c): Just deserts require the infliction of pain.

d): Justice is measured by the process.

e): The breaking of the law defines the offense.

The question of guilt is the hub of the entire criminal justice process.

Why are there such elaborate rules governing how to legally establish guilt?

There are elaborate rules governing how to legally establish guilt for several reasons:

1. Protecting the Rights of the Accused: The rules governing the legal establishment of guilt are designed to protect the rights of the accused, ensuring that they are not wrongfully convicted or punished for a crime they did not commit. This includes protections such as the presumption of innocence, the right to a fair trial, and the right to an attorney.

2. Ensuring Fairness and Impartiality: The rules governing the legal establishment of guilt are also designed to ensure fairness and impartiality in the criminal justice system. This includes rules such as the exclusion of evidence obtained through illegal means, the requirement of a unanimous jury verdict in criminal cases, and the requirement of a high standard of proof (beyond a reasonable doubt) to establish guilt.

3. Protecting Against Abuse of Power: The rules governing the legal establishment of guilt are also designed to protect against abuse of power by law enforcement and other authorities. This includes rules such as the requirement of a warrant or probable

cause for searches and seizures, and the requirement of Miranda warnings to inform suspects of their rights.

4. Maintaining Public Confidence in the Justice System: The rules governing the legal establishment of guilt are also important for maintaining public confidence in the justice system. When the rules are followed and a fair trial is conducted, it helps to ensure that the public perceives the outcome as just and legitimate, which is essential for the functioning of a democratic society.

Hence, the rules governing the legal establishment of guilt are an essential component of the criminal justice system, designed to protect the rights of the accused, ensure fairness and impartiality, prevent abuse of power, and maintain public confidence in the justice system.

Wherefore, once guilt has been established, concern about procedural safeguards and rights diminishes.

Even is a person is declared "not guilty," consequences are profound. Accused persons go to trial based on evidence presented by the police, although in some cases haphazardly. It seems to most that the accused is more than likely guilty of the crime alleged. After all, the district attorney must have had quite a load of proof on hand before making the decision to prosecute. A terrible stain is already cast upon a person. Even if the jury concludes that reasonable doubt exists as to guilt, this is an accusation that will be with that person for life.

The concept of guilt which guides the justice process is a narrow, highly technical one which is primarily objective or descriptive in nature.

In the legal system, offenses and questions of guilt are framed in terms much different from how the victim and the offender actually experience them.

a) The legal charge may seem to bear little relationship to the actual offense,

b) and the language of guilt or innocence may seem to have little connection to what actually happened.

When the legal charge sounds quite different from the actual offense, and the offender has been advised to plead "not guilty," many times the offender comes to believe that he is in fact not guilty.

In legal terms, what does the plea "not guilty" actually mean?

Is the way one says, "I want a trial," or "I need more time."

Social and behavioral scientists raise questions about the extent to which the offender is personally responsible, perhaps about the extent to which he is an offender rather than a victim.

Wherefore, the label of "guilty" sticks to a person for his entire life, and does become a part of his/her identity.

In Western culture, the basic assumption of human freedom and of personal accountability is important:

Even though the Apostle Paul confirmed that we have free will and the freedom to make choices, he also lamented that the power of evil can have a strong pull on our will and get us into trouble. In Romans 7:15, he said:

a) vs. 15a: I do not understand what I do.

b) vs. 15b: For what I want to do I do not do,

c) vs. 15c: but what I hate I do.

The Apostle Paul's problem isn't knowledge - he knows what the right thing is. His problem is a lack of power, how to do the right thing. He lacks power because the law gives no power.

In the very last days of Moses' life, when he was 120 years old, he made his farewell speech to the nation of Israel. Regarding the matter of free choice, what did Moses say are our two choices? (Deuteronomy 30:15):

a): See, I set before you today life and prosperity,

b): Death and destruction.

Israel had a choice: life or death, good or evil. It was up to them. God was going to glorify Himself through Israel one way or another. How it would happen was really their choice. It is still the same for us today.

Joshua took over as leader of Israel after the death of Moses, and in the final days of his life he too spoke about this matter of free choice. In Joshua 24:15, what did Joshua say were the two choices.:

a): Then choose for yourselves this day whom you will serve, whether the gods your ancestors served beyond the Euphrates,

b): Or the gods of the Amorites, in whose land you are living. What choice did Joshua make for himself and his family?

But as for me and my household, we will serve the Lord."

Joshua's bold statement indicates that he was determined to follow this course no matter what anyone else thought. His relationship with God was not based on any man, but on the Lord alone, and he would serve God no matter what anyone else thought or did.

a) Do you believe offenders should be held accountable for what they have done, regardless of background or circumstances, or do you believe we should take into consideration the social and economic roots and contexts of the crime as well.

Take into consideration the social and economic roots and contexts of the crime

b) Individuals background has an impact in one's decision, and we should not condemn them without knowing their back ground which may be the force to their wrong choices. Example, A person who was raised in a violent environment may be violent when he grows up.

I believe that every action that we take is accountable to some law whether it is the law of gravity, or a law of decency, or a law of the criminal justice system. If we cause harm to someone else or to someone's property, we should be held accountable for our actions.

The criminal justice system and our court systems were created to enforce the laws of accountability and responsibility. For those who refuse to be accountable, I believe these should be dealt with more severely.

In what way does the legal process discourage offenders from being accountable for or accepting responsibility for the choices between good and evil they have made? (Thought question - answers will vary.):

By giving them an option of making a not guilty plea. This makes and offender feels and believe in fact he/she is not guilt.

Being accountable for our own actions means that we would take responsibility for the outcome. If we were to jump off of a high wall, we would be accountable to ourselves for the fact that the laws of gravity will take over and bring us to the ground. If we act in a way that affects others, we must be held accountable for the effect that our actions had on them. However, many try to shift blame on to the parents, environment, mental illness, society etc.

Once guilt has been established, what is the second assumption that comes into play?

We assume that offenders must receive their "just deserts."

Just deserts, in the sense of "things deserved" has been used in the English language since at least the 13th century. Originally, it meant to get a reward for what had been done - whether good or bad. Similarly, "Let the punishment fit the crime" is a principle that means the severity of penalty for a misdeed or wrongdoing should be reasonable and proportionate to the severity of the infraction. The concept is common to most cultures throughout the world.

Criminal justice officials see their job as meting out appropriate levels of punishment.

What are a few of the rationales for delivering pain to the offender?

a): Pain. At some times we have done it in the name of treatment, as a means of rehabilitation.

b): Consequences. We administer pain in the name of deterrence, in fact, despite substantial questions about whether such deterrence actually works.

c): We administer pain in the name of deterrence despite questions about the morality of administering pain to one person for the purposes of possibly deterring another.

Because of this focus on inflicting pain, because of the threat of punishment, and because the punitive consequences are so serious:

a): elaborate safeguards of offenders' right are needed,

b): and these can make it difficult to get at truth.

c): Judges and jurors too may become less likely to convict when the potential punishment is seen as very severe.

Usually, the jury decides the facts of a case, but the judge determines the punishment. Some have suggested that judges alone should determine guilt in all cases. Juries are not technically trained in evaluating evidence. Additionally, judges are trained to recognize and suppress their own prejudices, evaluate information given to them, recognize prosecutorial strategy etc.

Studies of capital punishment have proven that the death penalty does not deters people from killing.

The threat to inflict pain on those who disobey has long been recognized as ...: basis of modern law.

The primary goal of our justice process is first the determination of guilt and once that is determined, the infliction of pain.

Appeals are usually centered on whether correct procedures have been followed.

With this emphasis on rules and process, priority is given to equity of treatment as a test of justice.

Due to stringent rules and regulations in the legal process, approximate equity in outcome is usually not achieved.

The criminal judicial system has become a huge bureaucracy with vested of its own.

What actually defines the offense and triggers the justice process?

The act of breaking a law, not the damage or conflict,

What weight or importance is given to social, moral, or personal factors?

Moral and social issues

Studies about the influence of economic factors on criminal behavior have attempted to link being financially deprived to increased motivation to commit crimes (especially property crimes). Other studies attempt to relate the involvement of criminals from poor neighborhoods to the distribution of power in society. The assumption in these studies is that criminal law is a tool used by the rich to advance their class interests. Studies of the relationship between unemployment and crime have also been used to explain away or excuse crime.

However, whatever the excuse or rationale, I believe a criminal should be accountable for his/her actions.

What are the five assumptions that we make about crime and justice?

There are many assumptions made about crime and justice, but five common ones are:

1. Crime is a violation of the law: This assumption states that crime is not just a violation of moral principles, but also a violation of a specific law or legal code that is designed to protect society from harmful behavior.
2. Crime is a rational choice: This assumption assumes that individuals who engage in criminal behavior do so after weighing the costs and benefits of their actions and deciding that the benefits outweigh the risks.
3. The justice system is impartial: This assumption assumes that the justice system is impartial and objective, and that it treats all individuals fairly and equally under the law.
4. Punishment deters crime: This assumption assumes that punishment, such as imprisonment or fines, deters individuals from committing future crimes by making them fear the consequences of their actions.
5. The justice system rehabilitates offenders: This assumption assumes that the justice system can rehabilitate offenders and help them change their behavior through programs such as counseling, education, and vocational training.

It is important to note that these assumptions are not always true in every case and that they have been subject to criticism and debate in the field of criminology.

a): Crime is essentially lawbreaking;

b): When a law is broken, justice involves establishing guilt;

c): So that just deserts can be meted out;

d): By inflicting pain;

e): through a conflict in which rules and intentions are placed above outcomes.

In criminal law, who is defined as the victim?

The State

Therefore, criminal law pits offenders against the State

Why are safeguards for the procedures so essential?

Because the state is so impersonal and abstract, forgiveness and mercy are nearly impossible to achieve.

Within our criminal justice system, why are forgiveness and mercy nearly impossible to achieve?

Because the state is so impersonal and abstract, forgiveness and mercy are nearly impossible to achieve.

Why doesn't the justice process include seeking reconciliation between the victim and the offender?

Because the relationship between victim and offender is not seen as an important problem.

This author contends that ours is essentially a retributive model of justice, and that model is at the root of many of our problems.

The idea that we should treat people as they deserve is commonly accepted. We do not think that war criminals should be allowed to live carefree lives after committing unspeakable crimes against humanity. However, there is a dangerous tendency to slip from retributive justice to an emphasis on revenge.

Sources:

Wharton, Francis. "Retributive Justice." Franklin Classics, October 16, 2018, ISBN-10: 0343579170.

Contini, Cory. "The Transition from Retributive to Transformative Justice: Transforming the System of Justice." GRIN Publishing, July 25, 2013, ISBN-10: 3656462275.

Husak, Douglas. "Overcriminalization: The Limits of the Criminal Law." Oxford University Press, November 30, 2009, ISBN-10: 0195399013.

Aston, Joseph. "Retributive Justice: A Tragedy." Palala Press, May 21, 2016, ISBN-10: 1358425558.

Hermann, Donald H.J. "Restorative Justice and Retributive Justice." Seattle Journal for Social Justice, 12-19-2017, https://digitalcommons.law.seattleu.edu/cgi/viewcontent.cgi?article=1889&context=sjsj.

CHAPTER VI
JUSTICE AS PARADIGM

Justice as Paradigm

Justice as a paradigm refers to the concept of justice as a fundamental framework for understanding and addressing social issues and inequalities. In this view, justice is not just a set of laws or rules, but a guiding principle that shapes our understanding of what is right and fair in society.

Justice as a paradigm recognizes that the concept of justice is complex and multifaceted, and that it extends beyond the legal system to encompass broader social, economic, and political structures. It acknowledges that social inequalities, such as poverty, racism, and discrimination, are deeply rooted in these structures and that addressing these inequalities requires a systemic approach.

In this paradigm, justice is seen as a transformative process that involves recognizing and addressing systemic injustices, promoting equality and fairness, and empowering marginalized communities. It is a process that requires active engagement and participation from all members of society, including individuals, communities, and institutions.

Accordingly, the justice as a paradigm approach emphasizes the importance of viewing justice not as a static concept, but as a dynamic and evolving framework that can guide us towards creating a more just and equitable society.

Restorative justice practitioners tend to agree that what truly makes a particular response to crime a "restorative" one is not so much a specific practice or process, but rather its adherence to a set of broad objectives that provide a common basis for the participation of par- ties in responding to a criminal incident and its consequences.

The objectives of restorative justice programs have been stated in a number of different ways, but essentially contain the following key elements:

(a) Supporting victims, giving them a voice, encouraging them to express their needs, enabling them to participate in the resolution process and offering them assistance. For the last twenty years or so criminal justice systems have been called upon to focus more directly on the needs and interests of victims. In 1985, the General Assembly adopted a Declaration of Basic Principles on Justice for Victims of Crime and Abuse of Power which stated that "informal mechanisms for the resolution of disputes, including mediation, arbitration and customary justice or indigenous practices, should be utilized where appropriate to facilitate conciliation and redress for victims". We now know much more about the needs of victims of crime and the ways in which the criminal justice system may address these needs (e.g., the need for information, participation, expression, empathy, redress, restoration of a sense of control and security, etc.).

Full text of the declaration is given below:

Declaration of Basic Principles of Justice for Victims of Crime and Abuse of Power

The General Assembly,

Recalling that the Sixth United Nations Congress on the Prevention of Crime and the Treatment of Offenders recommended that the United Nations should continue its present work on the development of guidelines and standards regarding abuse of economic and political power, Cognizant that millions of people throughout the world suffer harm as a result of crime and the abuse of power and that the rights of these victims have not been adequately recognized,

Recognizing that the victims of crime and the victims of abuse of power, and also frequently their families, witnesses and others who aid them, are unjustly subjected to loss, damage or injury and that they may, in addition, suffer hardship when assisting in the prosecution of offenders,

1. Affirms the necessity of adopting national and international measures in order to secure the universal and effective recognition of, and respect for, the rights of victims of crime and of abuse of power;

2. Stresses the need to promote progress by all States in their efforts to that end, without prejudice to the rights of suspects or offenders;

3. Adopts the Declaration of Basic Principles of Justice for Victims of Crime and Abuse of Power, annexed to the present resolution, which is designed to assist Governments and the international community in their efforts to secure justice and assistance for victims of crime and victims of abuse of power;

4. Calls upon Member States to take the necessary steps to give effect to the provisions contained in the Declaration and, in order to curtail victimization as referred to hereinafter, endeavor:

(a) To implement social, health, including mental health, educational, economic and specific crime prevention policies to reduce victimization and encourage assistance to victims in distress;

(b) To promote community efforts and public participation in crime prevention;

(c) To review periodically their existing legislation and practices in order to ensure responsiveness to changing circumstances, and to enact and enforce legislation proscribing acts that violate internationally recognized norms relating to human rights, corporate conduct, and other abuses of power;

(d) To establish and strengthen the means of detecting, prosecuting and sentencing those guilty of crimes;

(e) To promote disclosure of relevant information to expose official and corporate conduct to public scrutiny, and other ways of increasing responsiveness to public concerns;

(f) To promote the observance of codes of conduct and ethical norms, in particular international standards, by public servants, including law enforcement, correctional, medical, social service and military personnel, as well as the staff of economic enterprises;

(g) To prohibit practices and procedures conducive to abuse, such as secret places of detention and incommunicado detention;

(h) To co-operate with other States, through mutual judicial and administrative assistance, in such matters as the detection and pursuit of offenders, their extradition and the seizure of their assets, to be used for restitution to the victims;

5. Recommends that, at the international and regional levels, all appropriate measures should be taken:

(a) To promote training activities designed to foster adherence to United Nations standards and norms and to curtail possible abuses;

(b) To sponsor collaborative action-research on ways in which victimization can be reduced and victims aided, and to promote information exchanges on the most effective means of so doing;

(c) To render direct aid to requesting Governments designed to help them curtail victimization and alleviate the plight of victims;

(d) To develop ways and means of providing recourse for victims where national channels may be insufficient;

6. Requests the Secretary-General to invite Member States to report periodically to the General Assembly on the implementation of the Declaration, as well as on measures taken by them to this effect;

7. Also requests the Secretary-General to make use of the opportunities, which all relevant bodies and organizations within the United Nations system offer, to assist Member States, whenever necessary, in improving ways and means of protecting victims both at the national level and through international co-operation;

8. Further requests the Secretary-General to promote the objectives of the Declaration, in particular by ensuring its widest possible dissemination;

9. Urges the specialized agencies and other entities and bodies of the United Nations system, other relevant intergovernmental and non-governmental organizations and the public to co-operate in the implementation of the provisions of the Declaration.

ANNEX

Declaration of Basic Principles of Justice for Victims of Crime and Abuse of Power

A. Victims of Crime

1. "Victims" means persons who, individually or collectively, have suffered harm, including physical or mental injury, emotional suffering, economic loss or substantial impairment of their fundamental rights, through acts or omissions that are in violation of criminal laws operative within Member States, including those laws proscribing criminal abuse of power.

2. A person may be considered a victim, under this Declaration, regardless of whether the perpetrator is identified, apprehended, prosecuted or convicted and regardless of the familial relationship between the perpetrator and the victim. The term "victim" also includes, where appropriate, the immediate family or dependants of the direct victim and persons who have suffered harm in intervening to assist victims in distress or to prevent victimization.

3. The provisions contained herein shall be applicable to all, without distinction of any kind, such as race, color, sex, age, language, religion, nationality, political or other opinion, cultural beliefs or practices, property, birth or family status, ethnic or social origin, and disability.

Access to justice and fair treatment

4. Victims should be treated with compassion and respect for their dignity. They are entitled to access to the mechanisms of justice and to prompt redress, as provided for by national legislation, for the harm that they have suffered.

5. Judicial and administrative mechanisms should be established and strengthened where necessary to enable victims to obtain redress through formal or informal procedures that are expeditious, fair, inexpensive and accessible. Victims should be informed of their rights in seeking redress through such mechanisms.

6. The responsiveness of judicial and administrative processes to the needs of victims should be facilitated by:
(a) Informing victims of their role and the scope, timing and progress of the proceedings and of the disposition of their cases, especially where serious crimes are involved and where they have requested such information;
(b) Allowing the views and concerns of victims to be presented and considered at appropriate stages of the proceedings where their personal interests are affected, without prejudice to the accused and consistent with the relevant national criminal justice system;
(c) Providing proper assistance to victims throughout the legal process;
(d) Taking measures to minimize inconvenience to victims, protect their privacy, when necessary, and ensure their safety, as well as that of their families and witnesses on their behalf, from intimidation and retaliation;
(e) Avoiding unnecessary delay in the disposition of cases and the execution of orders or decrees granting awards to victims.

7. Informal mechanisms for the resolution of disputes, including mediation, arbitration and customary justice or indigenous practices, should be utilized where appropriate to facilitate conciliation and redress for victims.

Restitution

8. Offenders or third parties responsible for their behavior should, where appropriate, make fair restitution to victims, their families or dependants. Such restitution should include the return of property or payment for the harm or loss suffered, reimbursement of expenses incurred as a result of the victimization, the provision of services and the restoration of rights.

9. Governments should review their practices, regulations and laws to consider restitution as an available sentencing option in criminal cases, in addition to other criminal sanctions.

10. In cases of substantial harm to the environment, restitution, if ordered, should include, as far as possible, restoration of the environment, reconstruction of the infrastructure, replacement of community facilities and reimbursement of the expenses of relocation, whenever such harm results in the dislocation of a community.

11. Where public officials or other agents acting in an official or quasi-official capacity have violated national criminal laws, the victims should receive restitution from the State whose officials or agents were responsible for the harm inflicted. In cases where the Government under whose authority the victimizing act or omission occurred is no longer in existence, the State or Government successor in title should provide restitution to the
victims.
Compensation:
12. When compensation is not fully available from the offender or other sources, States should endeavor to provide financial compensation to:
(a) Victims who have sustained significant bodily injury or impairment of physical or mental health as a result of serious crimes;
(b) The family, in particular dependants of persons who have died or become physically or mentally incapacitated as a result of such victimization.
13. The establishment, strengthening and expansion of national funds for compensation to victims should be encouraged. Where appropriate, other funds may also be established for this purpose, including those cases where the State of which the victim is a national is not in a position to compensate the victim for the harm.
Assistance
14. Victims should receive the necessary material, medical, psychological and social assistance through governmental, voluntary, community-based and indigenous means.
15. Victims should be informed of the availability of health and social services and other relevant assistance and be readily afforded access to them.
16. Police, justice, health, social service and other personnel concerned should receive training to sensitize them to the needs of victims, and guidelines to ensure proper and prompt aid.
17. In providing services and assistance to victims, attention should be given to those who have special needs because of the nature of the harm inflicted or because of factors such as those mentioned in paragraph 3 above.
B. Victims of abuse of power
18. "Victims" means persons who, individually or collectively, have suffered harm, including physical or mental injury, emotional suffering, economic loss or substantial impairment of their fundamental

rights, through acts or omissions that do not yet constitute violations of national criminal laws but of internationally recognized norms relating to human rights.

19. States should consider incorporating into the national law norms proscribing abuses of power and providing remedies to victims of such abuses. In particular, such remedies should include restitution and/or compensation, and necessary material, medical, psychological and social assistance and support.

20. States should consider negotiating multilateral international treaties relating to victims, as defined in paragraph 18.

21. States should periodically review existing legislation and practices to ensure their responsiveness to changing circumstances, should enact and enforce, if necessary, legislation proscribing acts that constitute serious abuses of political or economic power, as well as promoting policies and mechanisms for the prevention of such acts, and should develop and make readily available appropriate rights and remedies for victims of such acts.

However, there remain frequent complaints that the formal criminal justice process ignores the victims' needs and wishes. By contrast, a restorative justice process is often uniquely suited to address many of the victims' most important needs. In particular, the formal justice process is not designed to allow victims to describe the nature and consequences of the crime, let alone to ask questions of the offender. The restorative justice model can support a process where the victims' views and interests count, where they can participate and be treated fairly and respectfully and receive restoration and redress. By participating in the decision-making, victims have a say in determining what would be an acceptable outcome for the process and are able to take steps toward closure.

Repairing the relationships damaged by the crime, in part by arriving at a consensus on how best to respond to it. In fact, it is often argued that the focus of the response should not be solely on the criminal incident, but rather on the relationships that it affected or damaged. Strengthening the com- munity can sometimes prevent further harm. A key feature of restorative justice is that the response to criminal behavior focuses on more than just the offender and the offence. Peacemaking, dispute resolution and rebuilding relationships are viewed as the primary methods for achieving justice and supporting the victim, the offender and for interests of the community. It can also be helpful for identifying underlying causes of crime and developing crime prevention strategies.

Denouncing criminal behavior as unacceptable and reaffirming community values. Denouncing certain behaviors is an objective of the restorative justice process just as it has been a fundamental objective of criminal law for centuries. However, the way in which the behavior is denounced is different. Denunciation is achieved in a more flexible manner, taking into account not only the rules, but also the individual circumstances of the offence, the victim and the offender. It is designed to be a positive denunciation within a larger process, rather than being the sole focus of the intervention. What the denunciation looks like and how it takes place during the restorative process will vary widely, but it remains an essential part of the process. At times, issues can obviously arise when the values that a given community reaffirms through the restorative justice process are not congruent with those enshrined in existing law.

Encouraging responsibility taking by all concerned parties, particularly by offenders. The restorative process is meant to make it easier for offenders to assume responsibility for their behavior and its consequences. A restorative process moves from merely assessing legal guilt to attempting to determine responsibility for a conflict and its consequences. Active acknowledgment and acceptance of personal responsibility for the crime and its consequences, rather than a mere passive one imposed by others, is what is being encouraged. Others who had a role to play in the offence or the circumstances that led to it are also encouraged to assume responsibility for their part in the incident. This has the effect of broadening out the process beyond the specific incident, victim and offender. The manner in which this responsibility will lead to action, in particular apologies and restoration, is left to be determined through the process itself and not through the automatic application of some general legal rules. At its best, the process may lead the offender not only to assume responsibility but also to experience a cognitive and emotional transformation and improve his or her relationship with the community and, depending upon the particular circumstance, with the victim and the victim's family.

Identifying restorative, forward-looking outcomes. Rather than emphasizing the rules that have been broken and the punishment that should be imposed, restorative approaches tend to focus primarily on the persons who have been harmed. A restorative justice process does not necessarily rule out all forms of punishment (e.g. fine, incarceration, probation), but its focus remains firmly on restorative, forward-looking outcomes. The restorative outcome that is being pursued is the repair, as far as possible, of the harm caused by the crime by providing the offender with an opportunity to make meaningful reparation. Restorative justice is relationship based and strives for outcomes that satisfy a wide group of stakeholders.

Reducing recidivism by encouraging change in individual offenders and facilitating their reintegration into the community. The past behavior of individuals and its consequences are clearly a central preoccupation of the restorative process, but so is the offender's future behavior. An offender's undertaking as it relates to his or her future behavior is usually an essential component of agreements arrived at through mediation or other restorative processes. Transforming or "reforming" the offender through the restorative process is a legitimate objective of the process and so is the prevention of recidivism. The insistence that offenders understand and accept responsibility for the consequences of their actions is clearly meant to affect the offenders' future behavior. It is understood that the community and statutory agencies have a role to play in this process.

Identifying factors that lead to crime and informing authorities responsible for crime reduction strategy. The restorative process is an open one that encourages frank discussion of the background of the offence in a spirit of explanation rather than making excuses. If, for example, this reveals that offenders come from areas with particular deficits, action can be taken to remedy the problem.

What we think we know as reality is often more complex and problematic than appears on the surface because modern psychology has revealed hidden motivations for what we do and think.

Hidden motivation is a kind of trigger that does not depend on any material reward such as money or success. It's something very internal that makes people do what they do. For example, if you want to win a competition, not because of the 1000 dollars prize, but because you want your family to be proud of you - that is hidden motivation, inter-alia, the reality has demonstrated that there are complex and overlapping layers of conscious and subconscious reality.

If an animal of known, stable genetic background is raised in a carefully controlled laboratory environment, and administered a precisely measured stimulus, the animal will respond as trained and expected.

What is a paradigm?

A particular way of constructing reality, and our retributive understanding of justice is one such construct.

In the most basic sense of the word, a paradigm is a framework containing all of the commonly accepted views about a subject, a structure of what direction research should take and how it should be performed.

Paradigms:

a) Shape: definitions of reality in a particular culture and era are ways of constructing reality.

b) Provide: the lens through which we understand phenomena.

c) Determine: how we solve problems.

d) Shape: what we "know" to be possible and impossible.

e) Form: our common sense, and things that fall outside the paradigm seem absurd.

It is not true that vast majority of the conflicts and harms that occur every day are handled through the legal system.

In civil procedures, person is pitted against person, rather than against State

What role does the state play in civil procedures?
Referee and arbiter.

Other than those two positions, the state plays no role in civil cases, unless the government launches a lawsuit or is the party being sued. Parties retain a lawyer - or may choose to represent themselves - to gather evidence and present the case in court.

Someone may ask, why are civil procedures less strictly regulated than criminal legal processes? It is because civil cases usually result in some form of compensation.

Two factors that might impact whether a criminal act will turn into a criminal case for the state.:

a): As status, race, and the ethnicity of the victim

b): Offender play a part,

a) In a civil procedure, the offense is considered to be against person

b) In a criminal procedure, the offense is considered to be against the State

What was the basic assumption of the Ptolemaic paradigm, which shaped Western thinking until the seventeenth century? Observed phenomena.

The basic assumption of the Ptolemaic paradigm, which shaped Western thinking until the seventeenth century, was that the Earth was the center of the universe, and all other celestial bodies, including the Sun and planets, revolved around it in perfect circles. This geocentric model was developed by the ancient Greek astronomer Ptolemy in the second century CE and was widely accepted in Europe during the Middle Ages and Renaissance.

According to the Ptolemaic paradigm, the Earth was viewed as the most important and significant body in the universe, and the motions of the planets and stars were explained in terms of their relation to the Earth. This view of the universe was reinforced by the dominant religious beliefs of the time, which held that God had created the Earth as the center of his creation and that humans were the most important and significant beings in the universe.

The Ptolemaic paradigm was challenged in the sixteenth and seventeenth centuries by astronomers such as Nicolaus Copernicus, Johannes Kepler, and Galileo Galilei, who proposed a heliocentric model of the universe in which the Sun, not the Earth, was the center of the solar system. This new paradigm marked a major shift in Western thinking about the nature of the universe and paved the way for modern scientific inquiry and discovery.

In early applications of the retributive model, punishment was severe.

a) There were no safeguards against abuse.

b) And no relationship between the severity of the offense and the punishment inflicted.

Prisons became popular as a way to apply proportionate punishment.

When was rehabilitation first included as a consideration in sentencing schemes?

The first half of the twentieth century.

What is one popular sanction that was introduced to relieve prison crowding?

Community service orders

The community service program allows inmates an opportunity to give back to the community while at the same time supporting the restorative justice initiative of making a contribution to society. These programs alleviate boredom and tension in prisons, resulting in a safer environment for both staff and inmates. Safer prisons help establish a sense of security within the communities and give offenders a sense of pride and accomplishment, as they provide needed services to various organizations throughout their community.

CHAPTER VII
COMMUNITY JUSTICE

Community Justice

Two developments in the history of "criminal justice" has historical interpretation tended to focus are the rise of public justice at the expense of private justice and an increasing dependence on prison as punishment. Furthermore, historical interpretation of criminal justice has tended to focus on two key developments:

1. The emergence of the modern criminal justice system: This development occurred in the eighteenth and nineteenth centuries and involved the establishment of formal institutions and procedures for enforcing the law, such as police departments, courts, and prisons. This period marked a shift from earlier forms of justice, which were often based on retribution and punishment, to a more rational and systematic approach to law enforcement.

2. The rise of rehabilitation as a key goal of criminal justice: This development occurred in the twentieth century and involved a shift in focus from punishing offenders to rehabilitating them and addressing the underlying causes of criminal behavior, such as poverty, addiction, and mental illness. This approach emphasized the importance of treating offenders as individuals and providing them with the support and resources needed to reintegrate into society and lead productive lives.

While these two developments have been important in shaping the history of criminal justice, it is important to recognize that there have been many other factors and influences that have contributed to the evolution of this field over time. These include changes in social and cultural values, advancements in technology and scientific knowledge, and shifting political and economic structures.

Texas and California tried two different incarceration policies, to see if time in prison or rehabilitation works better. Texas started imprisoning youth offenders with non-violent crimes for longer periods of time, hoping this would discourage other potential youth offenders from doing the same crimes. California took a different stance, putting their non-violent youth offenders in a rehabilitation center. According to the Center for Juvenile and Criminal Justice, the results for Texas showed that their stricter incarceration policy was unsuccessful and that non-incarcerated alternatives for youth were more effective.

Before the modern era, the offender and victim settled most disputes and wrongs outside of courts within the context of their kin and community.

The administration of justice was primarily a mediating and negotiating process rather than a process of applying rules and imposing decisions.

Jesus recommended a similar process in Matthew 18. What are the three steps Jesus said should be taken when a person offends you.:

a) vs. 15: If your brother sins against you, go and tell him his fault, between you and him alone. If he listens to you, you have gained your brother

It is essential that we go to the offending brother first - not griping and gossiping to others, especially under the guise of sharing a prayer request or seeking counsel. Instead, speak to the party directly.

b) vs. 16: But if he does not listen, take one or two others along with you, that every charge may be established by the evidence of two or three witnesses.

The circle of people in the situation only becomes wider as the offending party refuses to listen. It is also possible that the one or two more, after hearing both sides of the story, may resolve the issue by assigning responsibility differently than the first offended person had thought. The first one to plead his cause seems right, until his neighbor comes and examines him (Proverbs 18:17). The goal must always be the restoration of relationship rather than proving one's self right.

c) vs. 17: If he refuses to listen to them, tell it to the church. And if he refuses to listen even to the church, let him be to you as a Gentile and a tax collector.

So, if the matter cannot be resolved, i.e., if the offender does not repent and begin to make things right, what did Jesus say should be done next? (Matthew 18:17): tell it to the church. And if he refuses to listen even to the church, let him be to you as a Gentile and a tax collector.

Although we do not want to be unequally yoked with them, we should still treat our fallen brothers with great love, with the goal of eventually bringing about a full repentance and reconciliation.

Paul echoed the same drastic measure in 1 Corinthians 5:5, when he said: you are to deliver this man to Satan for the destruction of the flesh, so that his spirit may be saved in the day of the Lord.

The goal of the discipline is clear: the salvation, not the destruction, of a sinner's spirit. Though this man's conduct was clearly sinful, and needed severe correction, Paul does not write him off as forever lost. He believed that the effective use of church discipline may yet see him to salvation.

Vengeance as an option for satisfying the victim, family of the victim, or the community is always dangerous because it often led to reciprocal violence and blood feuds.

What people generally want from revenge is to:
- Restore their dignity, and increase their pride or stature.
- Restore the "honor" of the offended group by avenging the shame.
- Remember a loved one or ancestor. The slogan "September 11, 2001, we will never forget" is seen frequently and is used to sustain the war on terrorism.
- Teach a lesson to the aggressor,
- Punish people who cheat and break rules; ensure they learn their lesson.
- Act as a deterrent to predatory behavior,
- Obtain acknowledgement from the aggressor that they were wrong and they feel remorse,
- Obtain a sincere apology and know the aggressor is remorseful,
- Demonstrate their power so they no longer feel powerless,
- Obtain reparations; get paid back for their losses, and settle the score
- Make the aggressor suffer and feel their pain,
- Transform themselves from prey to predator, from powerless to powerful, and from shamed to proud,
- Tell their side of the story; set the record straight from their point of view.

Too often, the attempt to "get even" leads to prolonged and escalated violence.

What was available for the offender that limited vengeance for a period of time?

One option available for limiting vengeance for a period of time is the use of a statute of limitations. A statute of limitations is a law that sets a specific time limit within which a legal action must be brought. After the time limit has expired, the plaintiff is barred from bringing the action.

Statutes of limitations are designed to prevent the pursuit of old or stale claims, as evidence and witnesses may become unreliable or unavailable over time. They also provide a measure of certainty and finality, as potential defendants are not left with the threat of a lawsuit hanging over them indefinitely.

In criminal law, the use of a statute of limitations varies depending on the jurisdiction and the nature of the offense. Some jurisdictions have no statute of limitations for serious offenses such as murder or sexual assault, while others have shorter time limits for less serious offenses.

In civil law, the statute of limitations may vary depending on the type of claim being pursued. For example, in some jurisdictions, the statute of limitations for personal injury claims may be shorter than the time limit for breach of contract claims.

In summary, the use of a statute of limitations is one option available for limiting vengeance for a period of time in both criminal and civil law.

The passion and desire for revenge is strong and sometimes almost overwhelming. But our intuitive logic about revenge is often twisted, conflicted, parochial, and dangerous. Revenge is a primitive, destructive, and violent response to anger, injury, or humiliation. It is a misguided attempt to transform shame into pride - by whatever means, even violence.

Even still today, especially in gang related murders, the opposing gang will reciprocate with a vendetta - an on-going private feud where the members of the family of a murdered person seek to avenge the murder by killing the murderer or one of the murderer's relatives. When we lived in St. Thomas, the emergency room often became the scene of a battleground, where gangs would continue the fight because they knew family members would be present.

The sanctuaries in past times gave all the parties a "time out" to cool down.

During the Middle Ages in western continental Europe, what were some of the "official" courts in existence at that time?

a): State

b): Royal courts

c): Ecclesiastical, municipal,

d): Seigneurial authorities.

During the Middle Ages in Western Continental Europe, there were several "official" courts in existence, including:

1. Royal Courts: These were the highest courts of the land and were presided over by the king or his representative. They dealt with the most serious criminal cases, such as treason, and civil cases involving high-ranking individuals or the crown itself.

2. Ecclesiastical Courts: These courts were controlled by the Catholic Church and dealt with matters related to religious law, such as heresy and blasphemy, as well as matrimonial and testamentary disputes.

3. Manor Courts: These were local courts that dealt with civil disputes within a particular manor or estate. They were presided over by the lord of the manor and were responsible for enforcing local customs and traditions.

4. Town Courts: These courts were established in towns and cities to deal with local disputes and to enforce local laws and regulations.

5. Merchant Courts: These courts were established by medieval trade guilds and were responsible for regulating commercial activities and resolving disputes between merchants.

6. Feudal Courts: These were courts that were established by feudal lords to resolve disputes between their vassals.

7. Forest Courts: These were courts that were established to deal with disputes related to the use and ownership of forests and woodland areas.

Hence, during the Middle Ages, the court system was complex and varied depending on the jurisdiction and the type of case being heard.

What was the role of the court, once someone initiated prosecution?

Was to see that the parties cooperated.

Once someone initiates prosecution in a court, the role of the court is to impartially and fairly determine the facts of the case, apply the relevant law to those facts, and ultimately make a decision or judgement in the matter. This process involves several steps, which may include:

1. Pre-trial: Before a trial begins, the court may hold pre-trial hearings to determine issues such as the admissibility of evidence, the scope of the trial, and the availability of witnesses.

2. Trial: The trial is the main stage of the legal process, where the prosecution presents evidence and arguments to prove their case, and the defense responds with their own evidence and

arguments. The court hears testimony from witnesses, reviews evidence, and applies the law to the facts presented to make a determination of guilt or liability.

3. Sentencing: If the defendant is found guilty or liable, the court will determine an appropriate sentence or remedy, which may include fines, imprisonment, or other forms of punishment or compensation.

4. Appeals: If either party is dissatisfied with the court's decision, they may have the right to appeal to a higher court, which will review the case for errors in law or procedure.

Thus, the role of the court is to provide a fair and impartial forum for resolving disputes and administering justice. It is responsible for ensuring that the legal process is followed correctly, that the parties receive a fair hearing, and that justice is served according to the rule of law.

What were some of the factors that led to a reluctance to use the judicial option in medieval times?

There were several factors that led to a reluctance to use the judicial option in medieval times, including:

1. Cost: The legal process could be expensive, and many people simply could not afford to pursue a legal claim or defend themselves in court. This was especially true for peasants and other lower-class individuals who had limited resources.

2. Complexity: The legal system was complex and difficult to navigate, even for those who could afford to hire lawyers. Many legal disputes involved arcane points of law and complex legal procedures that were difficult for ordinary people to understand.

3. Corruption: Corruption was a problem in many medieval legal systems, with judges and other court officials often being open to bribery or other forms of influence. This meant that the outcome of a case could often be determined by factors other than the strength of the evidence or the merits of the arguments.

4. Fear of Retaliation: In some cases, individuals were reluctant to pursue legal action for fear of retaliation by the other party or their associates. This was especially true in cases involving powerful individuals or groups, such as feudal lords or wealthy merchants.

5. Lack of Trust: Many people simply did not trust the legal system or the courts to provide fair and impartial justice. This was especially true for marginalized groups such as Jews, Muslims, and other religious minorities who faced discrimination and prejudice in many medieval legal systems.

Accordingly, these factors led to a reluctance to use the judicial option in medieval times, with many people preferring to rely on informal methods of dispute resolution such as negotiation, mediation, or private arbitration.

As barbaric as we may think pre-modern justice was, traditional concepts of community justice recognized that ...:

a): harm had been done to people,

b): that the people involved had to be central to a resolution,

c): that reparation of harm was critical.

Restorative justice centers around the idea that because crime hurts, justice should heal. Conversations with those who have been hurt and those who have inflicted the harm must be central to the process. Surprisingly, victims of crime are often more concerned about emotional than material reparation. Lawyers are obviously not well trained to make a list of these emotional harms and how they might be healed. And so, the practice of restorative justice has become a de-professionalizing system. Lawyers still have an important role to play, but they are not in the spotlight as the person of most importance in a restorative justice system.

When did a series of changes begin to evolve, which would lay the basis for a drastically new approach to crime and justice? By the eighteenth and nineteenth centuries,

What did legal historian Harold J. Berman term this metamorphosis of the system for responding to crime and injuries?

Legal historian Harold J. Berman termed the metamorphosis of the system for responding to crime and injuries the "transformation of the Western legal tradition." Berman argued that this transformation took place over several centuries, beginning in the High Middle Ages and continuing through the Renaissance and the Enlightenment. During this period, the legal system underwent significant changes in response to social, economic, and political developments, including the rise of centralized monarchies, the growth of commercial trade, and the spread of humanist ideas about individual rights and freedoms. These changes led to the development of new legal concepts and institutions, such as the rule of law, the separation of powers, and the idea of individual rights, that form the basis of modern Western legal systems.

List of few of the many changes that were seen on the European continent.:

a): They began to claim the right to make new law and to abrogate old.

b): Formal, written law codes incorporating new principles began to replace custom.

c): The possibility of state intervention and initiative in certain types of cases.

d): On the European continent, prosecutors representing the state began to appear.

This process of changing the justice system evolved gradually over time, as representatives of the state insinuated themselves into the accusatorial process.

Overall, the justice system has expanded over time. It has also grown increasingly protective of individual rights and far more procedural in its application of the law (that is, far more demanding in its requirements of plaintiffs, lawyers, and law enforcement).

The development of this new legal system with central authorities occurred within the context of an overall struggle for power.

The struggle for power was between religious and secular authorities.

Roman law created the basis for canon law, which became the fundamental law of the church. Later its outlines were adopted by secular powers throughout all of western continental Europe.

Roman law was the legal system of ancient Rome, and the legal developments comprising more than a thousand years of jurisprudence from the Twelve Tables (c. 439 BC) to the Corpus Juris Civilis (AD 529) ordered by the emperor Justinian I.

Describe four features of Roman law when it was the legal system of ancient Rome:

a): Roman law was formal,

b): Rational,

c): Codified law based on logic

d): and fundamental principles.

Early Christian practice had focused on acceptance and forgiveness of wrongdoing, but canon law and the parallel theology which developed began to identify crime as a collective wrong against a moral or metaphysical order.

With the introduction of canon law, it became the church's business to purge the world of crime, which was believed to be a sin against not only an individual but also God. What three assumptions followed this perception?

a): The social order is willed by God

b): That crime is also a sin against this social order.

c): The church (and later the state) must therefore enforce that order.

What is the primary difference between community justice and state justice?

Community justice at its best represented negotiated, restitutive justice. State justice, however, is the king's peace. It is vertical, hierarchical, imposed, punitive.

The primary difference between community justice and state justice is their focus and scope. Community justice emphasizes the role of the local community in resolving disputes and addressing crime, while state justice places greater emphasis on the formal legal system and the state's responsibility for maintaining law and order.

Community justice seeks to involve members of the local community in the process of resolving conflicts and addressing crime. It is based on the idea that communities have the knowledge, resources, and capacity to respond to these issues effectively, and that involving community members in the process can help to build trust, promote accountability, and reduce recidivism. Community justice may involve informal mechanisms such as mediation, restorative justice, or community policing, as well as more formal processes such as community courts or diversion programs.

State justice, on the other hand, is focused on maintaining law and order through the formal legal system. It is based on the idea that the state has a responsibility to uphold the rule of law and to protect the rights and safety of its citizens. State justice involves the use of formal legal institutions such as police, courts, and correctional facilities to investigate, prosecute, and punish criminal offenses.

Accordingly, the primary difference between community justice and state justice is their focus on community involvement versus formal legal institutions, and their emphasis on resolution versus punishment. While both approaches are aimed at promoting justice and reducing crime, they differ in their methods and scope.

Below are some of the ways power was abused by the "state justice" system in the eighteenth century.:

a): Almost unimaginable forms of torture and punishment were commonplace—not only for duly-convicted criminals but for suspects and political enemies.

b): The crown claimed to be above the law,

c): the law was a crazy maze of custom and principle, logic and arbitrariness, special interests and public concerns.

In his book On Crime and Punishment, Cesare Becarria said that law should be:

a): be rationally rooted in the will of the entire community.
b): equally applied to all,
c): administered in a rational way by the state.

Becarria was of the opinion that people make decisions about their behavior on the basis of expectations about the pain and pleasure that will result from their choices.

When individuals make choices, they try to maximize their benefits and minimize their costs. In other words, people make decisions about how they should act by comparing the costs and benefits of different courses of action. As a result, patterns of behavior will develop within the society that result from those choices.

Eventually state justice was victorious. The result today, as Jerold Auerbach has so eloquently said.....:
a): Law is our national religion;
b): Lawyers constitute our priesthood;
c): The courtroom is our cathedral,
d): where contemporary passion plays are enacted."

At the core of the legal revolution was a movement from community justice to public justice.:

Newly-emerging governments were known to impose public, brutal punishments to serve as a symbol of their power, and as a way of asserting and dramatizing their power. However, this was nothing new. We have seen many examples of this in the Bible. Can you name one such example? (Thought questions - answers will vary.): We can see this at the time of John when he was at the Island of Patmos here, according to most biblical historians, he was exiled as a result of anti-Christian persecution under the Roman emperor Domitian.

What is one explanation for the fact that community justice had become less effective?

Community justice is an effort to reweave the fabric of community by forging a partnership between local governmental, the private sector, and community groups. This merger is intended to carry out functions that were once performed by the extended family, neighborhood, and school. The primary goal of community justice is to mobilize communities to be active partners in crime-control and problem-solving efforts.

However, many people work so many hours - they don't even know their neighbors, and don't have time to participate in such efforts.

Today's criminal justice system has not learned from the mistakes made through history, and has failed to established proper channels and balances of power, and finally has a system not in place that meets the needs of the offender, the victim, and the community.

CHAPTER VIII
COVENANT JUSTICE

Covenant Justice

Why is it so surprising that biblical justice offers a sharp contrast to retributive justice?

It may be surprising to some that biblical justice offers a sharp contrast to retributive justice because the concept of justice is often associated with punishment and retribution. Retributive justice, which seeks to punish wrongdoers for their actions and restore a sense of order and balance, has been a dominant approach to justice in many cultures and societies throughout history.

In contrast, biblical justice is grounded in the principles of compassion, mercy, and restoration. It recognizes that individuals who have committed harm or wrongdoing are not simply objects to be punished, but are human beings with inherent dignity and worth. Instead of seeking retribution, biblical justice seeks to repair the harm that has been done, restore relationships, and promote healing and reconciliation.

This approach to justice may be surprising to some because it challenges the traditional view that punishment is the only way to deter crime and maintain social order. It also emphasizes the importance of addressing the root causes of crime and social inequality, rather than simply punishing those who have committed wrongdoing.

Overall, the contrast between biblical justice and retributive justice highlights the importance of exploring different approaches to justice and recognizing the complexity and diversity of human experiences and needs.

Some passages in the Bible appear to be restorative. Others are definitely retributive. Below is a classification of the following verses.:

a) Exodus 22:1: Restorative

The Mosaic Law did not send a person to jail because of theft. Instead, the thief was simply required to restore what he stole, plus an additional penalty.

b) Leviticus 19:18: Restorative

Vengeance belongs to God (Romans 12:19) and we can actually hold back God's work of vengeance upon others by seeking it ourselves.

c) Numbers 15;30: Retributive

Such sin was not to be tolerated in Israel. This command was a cultural mechanism for addressing this sin, and ensuring that such arrogant flaunting of public morality would not be rewarded.

d) 1 Samuel 15:1-3: Retributive

e) Obadiah 1:15: Retributive

f) Matthew 5:39: Restorative

Now Jesus didn't mean that there is no place for punishment or retribution in society. Jesus here was speaking to personal relationships, and not to the proper functions of government in restraining evil (Romans 13:14). I must turn my cheek when I am personally insulted, but the government has a responsibility to restrain the evil man from physical assault.

g) Luke 19:8: Restorative

h) Romans 12:17: Restorative

This echoes Jesus' command in Matthew 5:38-45. We are to love our enemies and treat well anyone who treats us badly.

What two foundational concepts are essential if we are to begin to unravel biblical thinking about law and justice?

a): Shalom

b): Covenant

Two foundational concepts that are essential to unraveling biblical thinking about law and justice are:

1. Covenant: In the biblical tradition, a covenant is a binding agreement between God and his people. The idea of covenant is central to understanding biblical law and justice, as it establishes a relationship between God and humans that is based on mutual trust, loyalty, and obligation. The concept of covenant helps to frame the biblical understanding of justice as something that is rooted in God's character and purposes, and is designed to promote shalom (wholeness, peace, and flourishing) for all of creation.

2. Justice as righteousness: The biblical concept of justice is closely tied to the idea of righteousness, which refers to living in right relationship with God and others. The Hebrew word for justice, "mishpat," is often used in the Old Testament to describe the right ordering of relationships and systems, as well as the fair and impartial administration of the law. The concept of justice as righteousness emphasizes the importance of treating all individuals with dignity and respect, regardless of their status or position in society. It also emphasizes the responsibility of

individuals and communities to act justly and seek the well-being of others.

What are three dimensions, or applications, of shalom?

a): Material: Shalom usually refers to material or physical conditions or circumstances. God's intent is for humanity to live in physical well-being.

b): Physical conditions: Shalom has to do with social relationships. God intends for people to live in right relationship with one another and with God.

c): Circumstances: A third application or dimension of shalom in its biblical use applies to the moral or ethical realm.

What was one of the things that differentiated the Israelites so sharply from their contemporaries in the ancient Near East?

One of the things that differentiated the Israelites from their contemporaries in the ancient Near East was their monotheistic religion. While many of their neighbors worshiped multiple gods and goddesses, the Israelites believed in a single deity who was all-powerful and all-knowing. This belief in one God, known as Yahweh, was a central tenet of Judaism, the religion of the Israelites.

This monotheistic belief was not unique to the Israelites, but it set them apart from many of their neighbors who believed in a pantheon of deities. The Israelites also believed that their God had made a covenant, or special agreement, with them, and that they were his chosen people. This belief further reinforced their sense of distinctiveness and set them apart from other nations in the ancient Near East.

Accordingly, the Israelites' monotheistic religion was a key factor that contributed to their distinctiveness and set them apart from their contemporaries in the ancient Near East.

Covenant: Was the belief that God had made a covenant with people.

In the biblical milieu, what is a covenant?

Was a binding agreement made between two parties.

What is the central act of salvation, performed because of God's love, not because it was earned or deserved ….:

a) In the Old Testament? Was an act of liberation, the exodus from Egypt.

b) In the New Testament? A new day in relationships between God and humanity—and between persons—has been born.

What aspects of Hammurabi's law made it equivalent to state law?

It was hierarchical, imposed, punitive, rooted clearly in a distant and all-powerful king.

Hammurabi's law, also known as the Code of Hammurabi, was a set of laws and legal principles that were established by the Babylonian king Hammurabi around 1754 BCE. The code consisted of 282 laws that covered a wide range of topics, including criminal offenses, property rights, and commercial transactions.

There are several aspects of Hammurabi's law that made it equivalent to state law:

1. Uniformity: The code was uniform throughout the Babylonian empire and applied to all people living within its borders. This created a sense of consistency and predictability in the legal system, which was important for maintaining order and stability.

2. Authority: The code was established by a powerful king who had the authority to enforce it through the state's legal institutions. This gave the code a strong sense of legitimacy and authority, and helped to ensure that it was taken seriously by the people.

3. Publicity: The code was publicly displayed on a large stone monument, known as the stele of Hammurabi, which was placed in a public location. This made the code visible and accessible to all members of society, and helped to ensure that people were aware of the laws and their consequences.

4. Punishments: The code provided for specific punishments for specific offenses, which were enforced by the state's legal institutions. This helped to ensure that people knew the consequences of their actions and deterred them from committing offenses.

Hence, these aspects of Hammurabi's law made it equivalent to state law by establishing a uniform, authoritative, public, and enforceable legal system that applied to all members of society.

What aspects of Hebrew law made it intrinsically different from Hammurabi's law?

Hebrew law, as reflected in the Torah and the Talmud, is intrinsically different from Hammurabi's law in several ways:

1. Source of Law: Hebrew law is considered to be based on divine revelation, whereas Hammurabi's law was based on the authority of the king. In Hebrew law, God is the ultimate source

of law and authority, and the laws are seen as reflecting God's will and wisdom.

2. Ethical Principles: Hebrew law places a strong emphasis on ethical principles, such as justice, compassion, and righteousness, as well as legal principles. These ethical principles are woven throughout the legal code and are seen as guiding the interpretation and application of the law.

3. Treatment of Social Issues: Hebrew law also addresses social issues such as poverty, charity, and the treatment of widows and orphans, in addition to criminal and civil matters. This reflects a broader concern for the well-being of society as a whole and a recognition of the interdependence of its members.

4. Treatment of Women: Hebrew law provides greater protections and rights for women than Hammurabi's law, such as laws prohibiting the mistreatment of wives and daughters, and granting women the right to inherit property.

5. Focus on Individual Responsibility: Hebrew law places a strong emphasis on individual responsibility and accountability, rather than collective punishment. This is reflected in the principle of "an eye for an eye" which is often misunderstood as literal retaliation but is meant to emphasize proportional justice for individual wrongdoing.

Accordingly, these aspects of Hebrew law demonstrate a different approach to law and justice than Hammurabi's law. Hebrew law is based on a belief in a higher divine authority, incorporates ethical principles, addresses social issues, provides greater protections for women, and emphasizes individual responsibility.

Furthermore,

Hebrew law assumed that God was the source of all authority, above even kings.

And the New Testament supports this teaching. Romans 13:1-7 states, "Everyone must submit himself to the governing authorities, for there is no authority except that which God has established." The authorities that exist have been established by God. Consequently, he who rebels against the authority is rebelling against what God has instituted, and those who do so will bring judgment on themselves.

The question that follows is: "Is there a time when we should intentionally disobey the laws of the land?" The answer to that question may be found in Acts 5:27-29, "Having brought the apostles, they made them appear before the Sanhedrin to be questioned by the high priest.

'We gave you strict orders not to teach in this Name,' he said. 'Yet you have filled Jerusalem with your teaching and are determined to make us guilty of this man's blood.' Peter and the other apostles replied: 'We must obey God rather than men!' "From this, it is clear that as long as the law of the land does not contradict the law of God, we are bound to obey the law of the land. As soon as the law of the land contradicts God's command, we are to disobey the law of the land and obey God's law. However, even in that instance, we are to accept the government's authority over us. This is demonstrated by the fact that Peter and John did not protest being flogged, but instead rejoiced that they suffered for obeying God (Acts 5:40-42).

What are the two Hebrew words that are often translated into English as "justice"?

Sedeqah and mishpat.

The two Hebrew words that are often translated into English as "justice" are:
1. "Mishpat": This word refers to the administration of justice and the establishment of right relationships between individuals and groups. It is often used in the Old Testament to describe the legal and judicial system, as well as the fair and impartial administration of the law.
2. "Tzedakah": This word refers to the concept of righteousness, which encompasses the idea of justice, fairness, and compassion. It is often used in the Old Testament to describe acts of charity, generosity, and social justice, and emphasizes the importance of caring for the vulnerable and marginalized members of society.

Both of these words reflect the biblical emphasis on justice as something that is rooted in God's character and purposes, and is designed to promote shalom (wholeness, peace, and flourishing) for all of creation.

What meaning do these words carry?

Both have to do with righteousness, right-ordering, and making things right.

Match the following terms with the correct definitions.:
Social Justice ----- Retributive Justice ----- Biblical Justice:
a) Sees injustice of any kind, in any sphere, as contrary to shalom: Biblical Justice
b) Addresses wrongs having to do with the distribution of wealth and power: Social Justice

c) Addresses wrongs legally defined as crimes: Retributive Justice

Give a Biblical example not included in this text, where tit-for-tat justice was replaced by Biblical justice, an act of love based on need rather than merit. John 8:7 So when they continued asking Him, He lifted Himself up and said unto them, "He that is without sin among you, let him first cast a stone at her."

Like you, for my own example, I chose the woman caught in adultery, who should have been stoned. Under Jewish law, the witness to the capital offense was required to begin the stoning, to throw the first stone. When Jesus said, He who is without sin among you, let him throw the first stone at her, He was really saying, "All right, let's execute her. But let's do it right. The main witness has to have a hand in her execution." Now since adultery is a private act, it was almost never "witnessed" by anyone. In other words, the person who witnessed this act and reported it was probably the man who was laying with her. As a matter of fact, it was most likely a set-up. i think the guy(s) planned this event in advance.

Jesus' words implied that the man who committed the sin with her should be the one to throw the first stone. However, he was guilty of the same sin, deserved to die along with her - and he knew it very well. Actually, everyone there knew they had sinned. I imagine the oldest ones turned and walked away first. They had years and years of sins on their conscience. The younger ones were probably more prideful, and it probably took longer for the truth to sink into their minds. But eventually, they all realized they were guilty of sin and left Jesus alone with the woman. And He ministered to her with love.

Biblical justice shows a clear partiality toward those who are oppressed and impoverished.

It is false to believe that Biblical justice must begin with a forensic inquiry into wrongdoing to establish guilt, before attempting to right wrongs and find solutions.

Rather than being a set of imperatives, the Ten Commandments were intended as a pattern for living in covenant, in shalom.
Which sermon in the New Testament provides the pattern for living in shalom under the new covenant?

The Sermon on the Mount. Matthew 5

In God's eyes, it is the spirit of the law that matters, rather than the letter of the law. Jesus gave us a good example of this in Matthew 5:28, when He said: But I say to you that everyone who looks at a woman with lustful intent has already committed adultery with her in his heart.

It is important to understand that Jesus is not saying that the act of adultery and adultery in the heart are the same thing. Some people have been deceived on this point, and say "I've already committed adultery in my heart, so I may as well do it in reality." The act of adultery is far worse than adultery in the heart. Jesus' point is not to say they are the same things, but to say they are both sin, and both prohibited by the command against adultery.

We see this taught again in 1 John 3:15, when the Apostle John said:

Everyone who hates his brother is a murderer, and you know that no murderer has eternal life abiding in him.

To hate our brother is to murder him in our hearts. Though we may not carry out the action because of cowardice or fear of punishment, we probably wish that person was dead. Or, by ignoring another person, we might treat them as if they were dead. Hatred can be shown passively or actively.

Having eternal life in us is more than saying, "I am a Christian." But John says that one test to measure the proof of a genuine believer is the love test. Do we love our brother, or just put on a good front?

The Apostle Paul made this abundantly clear in 2 Corinthians 3:6, when he said: Who has made us sufficient to be ministers of a new covenant, not of the letter but of the Spirit. For the letter kills, but the Spirit gives life

The letter is the law in its outward sense, written on tablets of stone. The letter of the law came by the Old Covenant. It was good in itself, but it gave us no power to serve God or to change our hearts. It simply told us what to do. Paul says the letter kills because the law, exposing our guilt, "kills" us before God. It thoroughly and completely establishes our guilt.

Instead, the Spirit makes us alive to the letter of the law, fulfilling and completing the work of the letter in us.

d) Finally, in Romans 2:25-29, the Apostle Paul used a practical example to highlight how a person could keep the letter of the law and still transgress, because he/she does not keep the spirit of that same law in other areas. What example did he use? For circumcision indeed is of value if you obey the law, but if you break the law, your circumcision becomes uncircumcision. 26 So, if a man who is uncircumcised keeps the precepts of the law, will not his uncircumcision be regarded[a] as circumcision? 27 Then he who is physically[b] uncircumcised but keeps the law will condemn you who have the written code[c] and circumcision but break the law. 28 For no one is a Jew who is merely one outwardly, nor is circumcision outward and physical. 29 But a Jew is one inwardly, and circumcision is a matter of the heart, by the Spirit, not by the letter. His praise is not from man but from God.

Description of God's justice characters.: The character of God's justice, as revealed in the Bible, is multifaceted and complex. It is grounded in God's love, mercy, and compassion, and is designed to promote shalom (wholeness, peace, and flourishing) for all of creation.

Here are some key aspects of God's justice:

1. Restorative: God's justice is restorative, meaning that it seeks to repair the harm that has been done and restore right relationships. This is evident throughout the Bible, as God repeatedly calls his people to care for the vulnerable, seek justice for the oppressed, and work towards the well-being of all.

2. Merciful: God's justice is also merciful, meaning that it extends grace and forgiveness to those who have fallen short of his standards. This is evident in the biblical stories of individuals like David and Peter, who were forgiven and restored despite their failures.

3. Impartial: God's justice is impartial, meaning that it treats all individuals with fairness and equity, regardless of their status or position in society. This is evident in the biblical injunctions to care for the poor, the widow, the orphan, and the stranger, and to treat all individuals with dignity and respect.

4. Demanding: God's justice is also demanding, meaning that it holds individuals and communities accountable for their actions and calls them to live up to his standards. This is evident in the biblical injunctions to pursue righteousness and justice, and to resist the temptation to exploit or oppress others.

Hence, the character of God's justice reflects his deep concern for the well-being of all of creation, and his desire to see his people live in right relationship with him and with each other.

Shalom is possible only if we look out for the welfare of one another, even in wrongdoing.

In Luke 10:30-37, Jesus deepened and broadened the application of Shalom in the story of the Good Samaritan. In verse 30, what happened to a certain man? he fell among robbers, who stripped him and beat him and departed, leaving him half dead.

The verse said, "A certain man went <u>down</u> from Jerusalem to Jericho." The road down was a steep descent from Jerusalem to Jericho, which was about 18 miles east. It was called "the bloody way" and considered the most dangerous roadway of Palestine, because of robbers infesting the country.

Jericho was a priestly city. No less than 12,000 priests lived there who would frequently travel along "the bloody way" to minister in the temple in Jerusalem. The first two men passed by under the pretense of avoiding legal pollution, religious people bound by forms and rituals which they wouldn't break even to save a life. I wonder if another reason the first two men passed by was for the same reason people don't stop to help a victim today - for fear of also being attacked.

Jesus deepened and broadened the application of Shalom in the story of the Good Samaritan. List things which the Samaritan did for the injured man, in spite of their cultural differences, that the respected and religious men did not do. (There are actually 10 acts of kindness.):

a): Bound up his wounds,

b): Pouring on oil and wine.

c): Set him on his own animal

Despite his religious, cultural, and ethnic differences, the Samaritan reached out to meet the needs of the Jew.

d): Brought him to an inn and took care of him.

e): He took out two denarii and gave them to the innkeeper

There were actually 10 acts of mercy listed in this account. These actions illustrate for us exactly how we are to be a "neighbor.

Today's justice seeks to administer to each his or her just deserts to make sure that people get exactly what deserve.

a) With modern justice, the test of success is whether the proper procedures have been followed.

b) Biblical justice is measured by the substance, by the outcome, by its fruits.

Biblical justice focuses on right relationship not right rules. Highlight another difference between contemporary justice and Biblical justice, and explain the opposing mindsets here.:

a) Contemporary justice Our legal system defines offenses as violations of rules, of laws. We define the state as the victim.

b) Biblical justice in biblical terms, however, wrongdoing is not a contravention of rules but a violation of right relationships.

How has the restorative theme of Biblical justice been overwhelmed by the theme of retributive justice?

Developed as the result of a "historical short circuit" arising from the mix of biblical with Greco-Roman ideas.

Jesus' life and death on the cross was an attempt to move humanity toward shalom, toward the kingdom of God.
What proof do believers have that suffering love will be victorious over evil, and that good can triumph in the long run? Christ arose, and the resurrection.

God offers forgiveness because He loves us.

"For God so loved the world, that he gave his only begotten Son, that whosoever believeth in him should not perish, but have everlasting life" (John 3:16). God does not simply overlook our sin and say, "You're forgiven." God sees our sin but is ready to forgive us because Jesus fully took our sin on Himself and paid for our sin by His death on the cross. Our sin is serious and it cost Jesus incredible suffering. But from the moment we received Christ into our lives, His forgiveness is ours. We can't ever make up for our own sin or suffer enough for it – nor does God want us to. "But God demonstrates His own love for us in this: While we were still sinners, Christ died for us" (Romans 5:8.

God's actions throughout history demonstrate that his nature is indeed restorative. From the very beginning, God created the world with the intention of bringing shalom (wholeness, peace, and flourishing) to all of creation. When sin and brokenness entered the world through human rebellion, God did not give up on his creation, but instead initiated a plan of restoration that culminated in the life, death, and resurrection of Jesus Christ.

Throughout the Old and New Testaments, we see examples of God's restorative justice in action. He repeatedly calls his people to care for the vulnerable, seek justice for the oppressed, and work towards the well-being of all. He also extends mercy and forgiveness to those who have fallen short of his standards, and works to repair the harm that has been done.

For example, in the book of Exodus, God hears the cry of his people who are enslaved in Egypt, and intervenes to deliver them from their oppressors. In the book of Isaiah, God calls his people to act justly, care for the oppressed, and seek the well-being of all. In the New Testament, we see Jesus embodying God's restorative justice through his healing of the sick, feeding of the hungry, and forgiveness of sins.

Accordingly, the biblical narrative reveals a God who is deeply committed to the restoration of his creation, and who invites his people to participate in this work of justice and reconciliation.

CHAPTER IX
VORP VICTIM OFFENDER RECONCILIATION PROGRAM

VORP: An Experimental Plot

The Victim Offender Reconciliation Program (VORP) is a restorative justice process that aims to bring together victims of crime and their offenders in order to facilitate dialogue, repair harm, and restore relationships. VORP typically involves a trained mediator or facilitator who helps to facilitate the process and ensure that all parties are heard and respected.

The goal of VORP is to provide a safe and supportive environment in which victims and offenders can have a face-to-face meeting to discuss the crime that was committed and its impact on their lives. During the meeting, the offender takes responsibility for their actions, expresses remorse, and offers to make amends in some way. The victim is given an opportunity to express the harm that was caused, ask questions, and participate in developing a plan for how the offender can make things right.

VORP is based on the principles of restorative justice, which emphasizes the importance of repairing the harm that has been done and restoring relationships between individuals and communities. The process is voluntary for both victims and offenders, and participation is based on a mutual desire to work towards healing and reconciliation.

Overall, the VORP process provides a way for victims to have a voice in the criminal justice system, and for offenders to take responsibility for their actions and make amends for the harm that was caused. The process can be a powerful tool for healing and reconciliation, and has been used in a variety of criminal justice settings, including juvenile justice, adult criminal justice, and community-based programs.

The letters in the acronym "VORP" represent Victim Offender Reconciliation Programs.

The VORP process consists of ...: Face-to-face meetings between victim and offender to work out restitution.

VORP is a victim-driven program; the VORP process is fundamentally shaped by the victim's wishes. VORP caseworkers assist victims in identifying how the offense has affected them and what would be meaningful by way of reparation.

In the VORP process, what three elements are emphasized heavily?

In the Victim Offender Reconciliation Program (VORP) process, three elements are emphasized heavily. These are:

1. Dialogue: The VORP process emphasizes the importance of creating a safe and respectful space for victims and offenders to engage in dialogue. Through open and honest communication, both parties are encouraged to share their experiences, express their feelings, and listen to each other's perspectives.

2. Responsibility: The VORP process emphasizes the importance of offenders taking responsibility for their actions. Offenders are encouraged to acknowledge the harm that they have caused and to express genuine remorse for their behavior. This process can help offenders to understand the impact of their actions and to take steps to make amends.

3. Restitution: The VORP process emphasizes the importance of making amends for the harm that was caused. Offenders are encouraged to offer some form of restitution or reparations to the victim, such as paying for damages, performing community service, or participating in a treatment program. This process can help to repair the harm that was caused and to restore a sense of balance and justice to the situation.

Wherefore, the VORP process is based on the principles of restorative justice, which emphasizes repairing the harm caused by criminal behavior and restoring relationships between individuals and communities. By emphasizing dialogue, responsibility, and restitution, the VORP process provides a way for victims to have a voice in the criminal justice system, and for offenders to take responsibility for their actions and make amends for the harm that was caused.

What are some of the typical agreements that are reached through these meetings between the victim and offender?

a): Offenders may agree to work for victims.

b): Sometimes victims ask that offenders work for the community instead,

c): Offenders may sign a community service agreement.

d): They may agree to a certain behavior.

One outcome of the VORP process is a contract that identifies how the offender will make reparation for their actions. This contract may include:
- Monetary restitution for financial losses.
- Community service.
- A letter of apology.
- Some other meaningful step the offender can take to address the impact of his/her actions.

VORP seeks to work with offenders in repairing the harm they have caused. By fulfilling a VORP contract, an offender takes an important step toward doing this; it is a tangible and meaningful way to accept responsibility and move forward into a productive life.

Name the one benefit for each of the involved parties, resulting from these meetings, that seems the most valuable to you. The Victim Offender Reconciliation Program (VORP) process can provide numerous benefits for both victims and offenders. Here are some benefits for each party that seem the most valuable to me:

Benefits for Victims:
1. Empowerment: The VORP process can empower victims by providing them with a voice in the criminal justice system. They can express their feelings and opinions, have their questions answered, and participate in developing a plan for how the offender can make amends.
2. Healing: The VORP process can provide a sense of healing for victims by allowing them to confront their offender and express the harm that was caused. Through the process, victims can gain closure, move towards forgiveness, and work towards emotional healing.
3. Restitution: The VORP process can provide victims with a tangible sense of justice by requiring offenders to make amends for the harm that was caused. This can include financial restitution, community service, or other forms of reparations.

Benefits for Offenders:
1. Responsibility: The VORP process can help offenders take responsibility for their actions by acknowledging the harm that was caused and expressing genuine remorse. This can be a critical step in the offender's rehabilitation and can help them to avoid future criminal behavior.
2. Reintegration: The VORP process can help offenders to reintegrate into society by providing a sense of closure and

resolution. By making amends and restoring relationships with victims, offenders can move towards reintegration and can rebuild their lives.

3. Restoration: The VORP process can help offenders to understand the impact of their actions and to take steps to restore the harm that was caused. This can help offenders to rebuild their self-esteem and to become active members of their community.

Thus, the benefits of VORP are numerous and can provide a valuable alternative to traditional criminal justice approaches. By emphasizing dialogue, responsibility, and restitution, the VORP process can help to repair the harm caused by criminal behavior and to restore relationships between individuals and communities.

While only about one half of all referrals end in meetings, nearly all meetings result in Agreement

About 80 or 90 percentage of agreements are fulfilled after the meeting.

a) Does VORP change offender behavior? There is evidence to suggest that participation in Victim Offender Reconciliation Programs (VORPs) can lead to changes in offender behavior. While it is not a guarantee, research has found that offenders who participate in VORP are less likely to reoffend than those who receive traditional forms of punishment.

One reason for this may be that VORP allows offenders to take responsibility for their actions and make amends for the harm caused. By engaging in dialogue with their victims and making efforts to repair the harm, offenders may develop a greater sense of empathy and become more mindful of the consequences of their behavior.

Furthermore, the process of reconciliation can help to restore relationships and create a sense of community. By working together towards a common goal, victims and offenders may develop a deeper understanding of each other's experiences and perspectives, which can promote empathy and reduce the likelihood of future conflicts.

Overall, while VORP may not be a panacea for criminal behavior, it can be a valuable tool in promoting offender rehabilitation and reducing the likelihood of recidivism.

b) Pursuant to the study in the U.S. Midwest and 91 percent of offenders in a study in Langley, British Columbia, said that, if they had it to do over, they would go through VOC again. Offenders expressed an increased awareness of victims as people, and attitudinal change was measurable in some cases. This study shows that, offenders are willing to change, in contrast, same offenders shows that they will do a crime and are willing to participate in the VOC. offenses? A growing body of evidence suggests that restitution, including VOC, has an impact on recidivism as great as or greater than other sanctions.

Programs like VORP are being used increasingly in communities across the country and around the world. A 2001 Canadian analysis of 22 different studies involving 35 restorative justice programs found that participation in restorative justice significantly improved the likelihood of offenders complying with restitution agreements, compared to court-ordered payments.

Additionally, many studies have reported high levels of victim satisfaction from restorative justice processes that gave them the opportunity to tell the offender directly how they were affected and to be part of creating a restitution agreement.

Sentencings should contribute to the maintenance of a just, peaceful, and safe society by holding offenders accountable for their criminal conduct through the imposition of just sanctions which ...:

a): Denounce unlawful conduct and the harm done to victims or to the community that is caused by unlawful conduct

b): Deter the offender and other persons from committing offences;

c): Separate offenders from society, where necessary;

d): Assist in rehabilitating offenders;

e): Promote a sense of responsibility in offenders, and acknowledgment of the harm done to victims or to the community.

What are the five main things necessary to allow victims to restore their sense of worth and get on with their lives?

As an AI language model, I must clarify that the answer to this question may vary depending on the type of victimization and the individual circumstances of the victim. However, in general, here are five things that may help victims restore their sense of worth and move forward:

1. Supportive relationships: Victims may benefit from having supportive relationships with family, friends, or mental health professionals who can provide emotional support, validation, and understanding.
2. Access to resources: Victims may need access to resources such as financial assistance, legal representation, and healthcare services to help them recover from the harm they experienced.

3. Self-care: Engaging in self-care practices such as exercise, healthy eating, and mindfulness can help victims manage stress, anxiety, and other negative emotions that may arise from their victimization.

4. Empowerment: Helping victims regain a sense of control over their lives can be empowering. This can involve assisting them in setting achievable goals and taking steps to achieve them.

5. Justice and accountability: In cases where the victimization involved a crime, holding the perpetrator accountable and seeking justice may help the victim feel validated and restored in their sense of worth. This may involve reporting the crime, participating in legal proceedings, and receiving restitution.

What is the primary focus of the VORP process? The Victim Offender Reconciliation Program, which involves victim-offender reconciliation and offender restitution, involves the steps of referral, client intake, assignment to a volunteer, mediation, and monitoring.

Name a couple of the secondary benefits that may also be seen along the way?

a): That the personal accountability that VOC offers can change offenders— attitudes and behavior.

b): It will help to reform the offenders

VORP has become the agent of a transformation of my understanding of justice and a demonstration that such justice is not just theoretical but can be practical.

Since 1974, VORP has served as both an experimental and a demonstration plot.

Why is the church's role critical in planting and nursing the VORP movement? now, the church played a pivotal role in its development and spread and still remains deeply involved in many communities.

Restorative advocates in a church can demonstrate the Biblical basis for restoration. Church leaders should attend restorative programs and training. The leaders should then train volunteers in the church and organize their own restorative programs. There should be committees in the church focused on local community needs, stepping in to help in the aftermath of a crime.

CHAPTER X
A RESTORATIVE METAPHOR

A Restorative Metaphor

A common metaphor used in restorative practices is that of a broken relationship being like a broken vase. The idea is that when a relationship is damaged or broken, it is similar to a vase that has been shattered into many pieces. To repair the relationship or the vase, it requires time, patience, and effort to carefully pick up each piece, examine it, and determine where it fits in the larger picture.

Similarly, in restorative practices, the process of repairing a relationship involves carefully examining the harm that was caused, identifying the needs of all parties involved, and working together to rebuild the relationship piece by piece. The goal is not just to repair the damage but to create a new, stronger relationship that is built on mutual understanding, respect, and trust. This process requires everyone involved to be committed to the work of restoration, to communicate openly and honestly, and to be willing to take responsibility for their actions and make amends where necessary. Just like a restored vase can be even more beautiful than it was before, a restored relationship can be even stronger and more meaningful than it was before the harm occurred.

In the framework of criminal justice and restorative justice, the metaphor we look through determines both the problem and the solution.

The criminal justice process views crime through a retributive metaphor.

What does justice require in the retributive vs. the restorative "metaphor"?

a) Retributive Justice: a system of criminal justice based on the punishment of offenders rather than on rehabilitation. Justice determines blame and administers pain in a contest between the offender and the state directed by systematic rules.

Broadly speaking, all crime is against the state, or government, insofar as it disturbs the public order and tranquility. But there are three criminal activities that are directed against the existence of the state itself: treason, sedition, and rebellion.

b) Restorative Justice: a system of criminal justice which focuses on the rehabilitation of offenders through reconciliation with victims and the community at large. Justice involves the victim, the offender, and the community in a search for solutions which promote repair, reconciliation, and reassurance.

Crime affects our sense of trust, resulting in feelings of suspicion of estrangement, and sometimes of racism.

Crime is, at its core, a violation of a person by another person who himself or herself may be wounded.

What are some of the dangers in re-labeling crime simply as "conflict"?

Re-labeling crime simply as "conflict" can be dangerous because it downplays the severity of criminal behavior and undermines the importance of holding individuals accountable for their actions. Some of the specific dangers of re-labeling crime as conflict include:

1. Lack of Accountability: When criminal behavior is labeled as "conflict," there is a risk that individuals who engage in such behavior will not be held accountable for their actions. This can create a sense of impunity, where individuals feel free to engage in criminal behavior without fear of consequences.

2. Undermining Justice: If criminal behavior is not properly labeled as such, it can undermine the principles of justice and fairness. Victims may not receive the justice they deserve, and society as a whole may lose faith in the legal system.

3. Inadequate Resources: If crime is re-labeled as "conflict," there is a risk that resources for addressing criminal behavior will be inadequate. This could lead to a lack of funding for law enforcement, criminal justice systems, and victim services, which could have serious consequences for public safety.

4. Normalizing Violence: If criminal behavior is labeled as "conflict," it can normalize violence and aggression. This can have a detrimental effect on social norms and values, and could contribute to an increase in violent behavior in society.

Hence, re-labeling crime as "conflict" can be dangerous because it downplays the seriousness of criminal behavior, undermines the principles of justice and fairness, creates a sense of impunity, and may lead to inadequate resources for addressing criminal behavior. Furthermore,

In situations of domestic violence, for example, we have too often defined violent acts with serious consequences as simply an outgrowth of conflict. This has tended to mute responsibility for behavior by blaming the victim. It also assumes that violence is simply an escalation of conflict.

What are some of the dangers in re-labeling crime as "problematic situations"?

But problematic situations feel vague and, for serious harms, may seem to minimize the dimensions of the hurt. Certainly, it is difficult to imagine problematic situations taking the place of crime in ordinary discussion!

What are the four basic dimensions of harm that come about as a result of a crime?

The four basic dimensions of harm that can result from a crime are:

1. Material or economic harm: This type of harm involves the loss of property or financial resources as a result of the crime. It includes damages to physical property, theft, and loss of income.
2. Emotional or psychological harm: This type of harm refers to the emotional or psychological impact that the crime has on the victim. It can include trauma, anxiety, depression, fear, and loss of trust or sense of safety.
3. Social harm: This type of harm affects the victim's relationships and interactions with others. It can include isolation, stigma, discrimination, and damage to the victim's reputation or social status.
4. Physical harm: This type of harm involves bodily injury or harm to physical health as a result of the crime. It can range from minor injuries to serious and life-threatening physical harm.

It is important to note that victims of crime may experience harm in multiple dimensions, and that the harm may have long-lasting effects on their lives. Recognizing and addressing these different dimensions of harm is important in supporting victims in their recovery and in holding perpetrators accountable for their actions.

Who is defined as the victim in the retributive vs. the restorative "metaphor"?

a) Retributive Justice: the state as victim,

b) Restorative Justice: people as victims

In the retributive metaphor, the victim is often seen as a passive participant in the criminal justice system. The focus is primarily on punishing the offender for their wrongdoing, with less emphasis on meeting the needs of the victim. The victim may be viewed as a witness to the crime, rather than an active participant in the process.

In contrast, in the restorative metaphor, the victim is seen as a key participant in the process of addressing harm caused by the crime. The focus is on repairing the harm and addressing the needs of all parties involved, including the victim, the offender, and the community. The victim is an active participant in the process, with a voice and a role in determining how the harm can be repaired and what actions the offender can take to make amends.

Therefore, the difference between the two metaphors lies in the role and involvement of the victim. In the retributive metaphor, the victim is often viewed as a passive observer, while in the restorative metaphor, the victim is seen as an active participant in the process of repairing harm and restoring relationships.

What is the definition of crime in the retributive vs. the restorative "metaphor"?

The definition of crime in the retributive metaphor versus the restorative metaphor is different.

In the retributive metaphor, crime is seen as an offense against the state and the law, and the focus is on punishing the offender for their wrongdoing. The offender is seen as having violated the law and must be held accountable through sanctions, such as imprisonment or fines. The retributive metaphor is rooted in a traditional criminal justice system that emphasizes punishment and retribution.

In contrast, the restorative metaphor defines crime as an offense against individuals and communities, and the focus is on repairing the harm caused by the offense. The offender is seen as having caused harm and is encouraged to take responsibility for their actions, make amends, and engage in a process of healing and reconciliation with the victim and the community. The restorative metaphor emphasizes repairing the harm caused by the offense and restoring relationships between the offender, victim, and community.

Thus, the retributive metaphor defines crime in terms of a violation of the law and the need for punishment, while the restorative metaphor defines crime in terms of harm caused to individuals and communities and the need for healing and restoration.

a) Retributive Justice: Crime defined by violation of rules (i.e., broken rules)

b) Restorative Justice: Crime defined by harm to people and relationships (i.e., broken relationships)

The Bible holds out for us a vision of how people ought to live together in a state of right relationship.

Psalm 133:1 says, "Behold, how good and how pleasant it is for brethren to dwell together in unity!" This verse expresses the goal, the hope, the prayer of all Christians. What a great thing it would be if all the people could live together harmoniously! What things we could accomplish! What great pleasure we would have! How attractive that would be.

This is a prophecy about our future. Isaiah 11:6 says, "The wolf also shall dwell with the lamb, and the leopard shall lie down with the kid; and the calf and the young lion and the fatling together; and a little child shall lead them. And the cow and the bear shall feed; their young ones shall lie down together: and the lion shall eat straw like the ox. And the sucking child shall play on the hole of the asp, and the weaned child shall put his hand on the cockatrice' den. They shall not hurt nor destroy in all my holy mountain: for the earth shall be full of the knowledge of the LORD, as the waters cover the sea."

When the Messiah reigns, nature will be transformed. No longer will there be predators among the animals, and seemingly all animals will be only herbivores (the cow and the bear shall graze . . . the lion shall eat straw like the ox). Not only will the way animals relate to each other be changed, but the way they relate to humans will be changed. A little child will be safe and able to lead a wolf or a leopard or a young lion or a bear. Even the danger of predators like cobras and vipers will be gone.

To be Biblical in our understanding, we will have to see injustice holistically, without artificial lines between crimes and other injustices.

When a wrong or crime occurs, what should be the central question? What should be done to the offender?

When a wrong or crime occurs, the central question should be: "How can we repair the harm caused by this offense and prevent it from happening again in the future?"

This question shifts the focus from punishment and retribution to repairing harm and restoring relationships. It acknowledges the harm caused to individuals and communities by criminal behavior and recognizes the importance of addressing the underlying issues that contribute to crime.

By prioritizing the repair of harm and prevention of future offenses, this question encourages a restorative justice approach that seeks to promote healing, accountability, and reconciliation. It also emphasizes the importance of addressing the root causes of crime, such as poverty, inequality, and social injustice.

Overall, the central question should not just be about assigning blame or punishment, but rather about how to address the harm caused by the offense and prevent it from happening again in the future.

List of four goals of justice that would meet this need.:

a): justice must go beyond a return to the status quo.

b): True justice cannot occur unless people and relationships are transformed into something that is healthy so the injury does not recur.

c): Justice may mean moving in a new direction rather than returning to the situation of the past.

d): Justice may involve more than filling a hole and leveling it off. The hole may need to be heaped up until it overflows.

2nd Corinthians 5 makes a link between reconciliation and new creation. Paul used words derived from the root word "reconcile" five times in verses 18-20. Type the phrases where you find these words.:

a) vs. 18a: who hath reconciled us to himself by Jesus Christ,

God has initiated this ministry of reconciliation, even though He is the innocent party. He reconciled us to Himself; we did not reconcile ourselves to Him.

b) vs. 18b: and hath given to us the ministry of reconciliation

Having has reconciled us to Himself through Jesus Christ, now God expects us to take up the ministry of reconciliation, and has therefore committed to us the word of reconciliation.

c) vs. 19c: reconciling the world unto himself

Through all the terrors of the cross, God the Father was working in and with God the Son, reconciling the world to Himself. The Father and the Son worked together on the cross.

d) vs. 19e: and hath committed unto us the word of reconciliation.

Why? Because God has gone soft, and given mankind a "Get Out of Hell Free" card? Not at all. Instead, it is because our trespasses were imputed to Jesus. The justice our sin demanded is satisfied, not excused.

e) vs. 20d: be ye reconciled to God.

What did the Apostle Paul consider to be his role in this ministry of reconciliation? (vs. 20): we are ambassadors for Christ.

The Apostle Paul considered himself to be an ambassador of Christ and a minister of reconciliation. In 2 Corinthians 5:18-19, he wrote: "All this is from God, who through Christ reconciled us to himself and gave us the ministry of reconciliation; that is, in Christ God was reconciling the world to himself, not counting their trespasses against them, and entrusting to us the message of reconciliation."

Paul saw his role as bringing people to reconciliation with God through Jesus Christ, and also promoting reconciliation between individuals and within communities. He believed that Christ's death and resurrection had reconciled humanity to God, and that this reconciliation could be extended to all people through the preaching of the gospel.

In addition, Paul emphasized the importance of reconciling relationships between individuals and within communities. He urged believers to forgive one another, to live in harmony with one another, and to seek to build up the body of Christ. He also challenged social norms and structures that perpetuated injustice and inequality, and called on Christians to work for social justice and reconciliation.

Accordingly, Paul's view of his role in the ministry of reconciliation was grounded in the belief that God had reconciled humanity to himself through Christ, and that this reconciliation could be extended to all people through preaching the gospel and working for reconciliation between individuals and communities.

An ambassador does not speak to please his audience, but the King who sent him. An ambassador does not speak on his own authority; his own opinions or demands mean little. He simply says what he has been commissioned to say. But an ambassador is more than a messenger; he is also a representative, and the honor and reputation of his country are in his hands.

Paul understood that he was serving in a foreign land as the representative of a King. The King had a message, and Paul delivered that message as though God were pleading through him.
Justice which aims to fill and overflow must begin by identifying and seeking to meet human needs.

When there has been a crime, the starting point for justice must begin with ...: the needs of the person violated.
What are just a few of the needs of the victim?

a): Victims need someone to listen to them.

b): They must have opportunities to tell their story and to vent their feelings, perhaps over and over.

c): They must tell their truth.

d): they need others to suffer with them, to lament with them the evil that has been done.

If you are counseling the victim of a crime, following are a few keys you can suggest that may help this person recover emotionally:

- <u>Take care of your thoughts</u>. You will have to make sure that you spend more time thinking about good things than the situation. Your thoughts have direct access to your emotions. If you think about unpleasant things for a long time, you may damage your ability to enjoy your life permanently! Philippians 4:8 gives us the perfect guideline in this: "Finally, brothers, whatever is true, whatever is noble, whatever is right, whatever is pure, whatever is lovely, whatever is admirable--if anything is excellent or praiseworthy--think about such things."

- <u>Take care of the words you speak</u>. When somebody talks to you, avoid talking like a victim. Talk positive, not negative. Talk life, not death. What we say makes a difference in our lives. Our words are the keys to abundant life. Unlock the door to your life of abundance by keeping a watch on what you say. Proverbs 18;21 says, "Death and life are in the power of the tongue: and they that love it shall eat the fruit thereof."

- <u>Take care of your self-talk</u>. Self-talk is the conversation with yourself that is going on in your mind all the time. Negative self-talk can lead to low self-esteem, create a myriad of health problems brought on by needless anxiety and stress and also will result in causing you to underachieve in life. Instead, follow the advice of Ephesians 5:19: "Speaking to yourselves in psalms and hymns and spiritual songs, singing and making melody in your heart to the Lord."

- <u>Take care of your body language</u>. If you walk like you are depressed or afraid, you will start to feel depressed or afraid. Hold your head straight up! This action has a psychological background! Good posture and a jaunty step raise your mood and improves your impression on other people. Spiritual caregivers are being trained to convince potential suicide victims to look up to the ceiling, because this helps immediately to feel better. Mind and posture influence each other more than you can imagine.

- <u>Take care of your boundaries</u>. When victims continue to act like victims, it has been proven that people will advantage of that. Do not allow other people to do things to you than you don't want, or manipulate you into doing things that you don't want to do. If you do not want to do something, look the other person straight in the eyes, leave no doubt that you understood everything and then say NO.

- <u>Take care of your faith</u>. Your faith in God, and your faith in the basic goodness of other people, may have taken a hit. Spend time in the Word, soaking up His affirmations of how precious you are to Him. Memorize His promises. Make index cards with "fear not" verses, and put them in strategic positions. My favorite verse is Isaiah 41:10: "Fear thou not; for I am with thee: be not dismayed; for I am thy God: I will strengthen thee; yea, I will help thee; yea, I will uphold thee with the right hand of my righteousness."

What is the real value and importance of restitution?

Its real importance is symbolic. Restitution implies an acknowledgment of the wrong and a statement of responsibility.

The real value and importance of restitution lies in its ability to repair the harm caused by a crime or wrongdoing and promote accountability and responsibility.

Restitution is a form of reparative justice that requires the offender to make amends for the harm they have caused to the victim and/or the community. This can take many forms, such as paying for damages, returning stolen property, or performing community service.

By requiring the offender to make restitution, the focus shifts from punishment and retribution to repairing the harm caused by the offense. This approach emphasizes the importance of holding offenders accountable for their actions and promoting responsibility and remorse.

Restitution also has practical benefits. It can help to compensate the victim for their losses and restore their sense of justice and dignity. It can also reduce the financial burden on the criminal justice system and the community by allowing the offender to make amends directly.

Thus, the real value and importance of restitution lies in its ability to promote healing and restoration for victims and communities, encourage accountability and responsibility in offenders, and reduce the burden on the criminal justice system.

What are the basic differences between "complete freedom" and "complete order"?

a) Complete Freedom: at least in the sense of freedom to do whatever we wish without formal or informal controls, would likely be chaotic and unsafe, a Hobbesian world.

b) Complete Order: on the other hand, even if it were attainable, would come at the price of freedom.

The basic differences between "complete freedom" and "complete order" can be understood as follows:

Complete freedom refers to a situation in which individuals are allowed to act without any constraints or limitations. This means that people have the ability to make their own choices and decisions, and are free to pursue their own interests and goals without interference from external sources. In a society that values complete freedom, individuals have the right to express themselves, assemble freely, and engage in activities that may be considered controversial or even offensive to others.

On the other hand, complete order refers to a situation in which there is strict control and regulation of individual behavior. In a society that values complete order, the government or other governing bodies have the authority to set rules and regulations that govern people's actions, and to enforce these rules through various means, such as law enforcement or other forms of social control. The emphasis is on maintaining stability and security, rather than on individual freedom of expression.

While complete freedom and complete order represent opposite ends of a spectrum, in reality, most societies strike a balance between the two. This balance can vary depending on a range of factors, such as cultural values, political ideology, and historical context. A well-functioning society seeks to balance individual freedom with social order, recognizing that both are important for the well-being and flourishing of individuals and communities.

What are some of the informal controls that can help maintain order in society?

Informal controls are unwritten rules, norms, and customs that guide behavior in society. These controls are not enforced by the government or other formal institutions, but instead rely on social pressure, expectations, and voluntary compliance. Some examples of informal controls that can help maintain order in society include:

1. Social norms: Norms are unwritten rules that govern behavior in society. They are often based on shared values and beliefs, and are reinforced through social pressure and expectations.

For example, the norm of respecting other people's property helps maintain order by discouraging theft and vandalism.

2. Reputation: A person's reputation can influence how others perceive and interact with them. People may avoid behaving in ways that could damage their reputation, or may seek to enhance their reputation through positive actions. This can help encourage prosocial behavior and discourage antisocial behavior.

3. Peer pressure: Peer pressure can be a powerful force in shaping behavior. People may conform to the behavior of their peers in order to fit in, or may be encouraged to behave in certain ways by their social group. This can be positive, such as when peers encourage each other to study or engage in healthy activities, or negative, such as when peers pressure each other to engage in risky or illegal behaviors.

4. Family and community values: Family and community values can play an important role in guiding behavior. These values are often passed down through generations and can help shape attitudes and beliefs about what is acceptable behavior. For example, a strong emphasis on family values may discourage behaviors such as drug use or delinquency.

5. Self-regulation: Individuals may choose to regulate their own behavior based on their own moral or ethical principles. This can help promote self-control and responsible behavior, and may be reinforced by a sense of guilt or shame when one's actions are perceived as harmful to others.

Accordingly, informal controls can play an important role in maintaining order in society by encouraging prosocial behavior, discouraging antisocial behavior, and promoting a sense of responsibility and accountability among individuals.

Which is easier? Making things right

a) Punishment for crime sends the message to offenders: Do not commit offenses because they are against the law.

b) Reparation or restitution sends the message to offenders: Don't commit offenses because it harms someone. Those who harm others will have to make it right.

It is not true when an offender participates in the process of reparation or restitution, the message that this is necessary because someone was harmed always sinks in.

We can denounce crime more constructively by doing things for the victim (and requiring offenders to do so), rather than ...: against the offender.

What are just a few of the needs of the offender?

a): They need to have their stereotypes and rationalizations' their misattributions—about the victim and the event challenged.

b): They may need to learn to be more responsible.

c): They may need to develop employment and interpersonal skills.

d): They often need emotional support.

The victim's needs should be a starting point, but that the offender's needs are of equal concern. In the aftermath of crime, victims' needs form the starting point for restorative justice. But one must not neglect offender and community needs.

In God's eyes, everyone is of equal importance. In Acts 10:34, the Apostle Peter said, "Of a truth I perceive that God is no respecter of persons."

Our human nature makes us want to shut the criminal down and give them "what they deserve." In our society, the offender doesn't seem like a person who would deserve any special consideration. But thank God, He doesn't see the crime - He only sees the heart. God doesn't see economic status - He only sees the heart. He doesn't see nationality or race - He only sees the heart. He doesn't see our past offenses - He sees our heart, our repentance, our willingness to make things right. I believe it is just as important to lead an offender to a saving relationship with God so he will want to do good and make things right, as it is to make things right for the victim.

How does Judge Chaleen implement responsible sentencing in his courtroom? he tells offenders the dimensions they must address. Then he tells them to come back with a proposal on how they expect to meet these requirements and how the sentence will be monitored and enforced.

What do you consider to be an important difference in the view of accountability in the retributive vs. the restorative: Offenders must be held accountable, but so too must society. Society must be accountable to victims, helping to identify and meet their needs. Likewise, the larger community must attend to the needs of offenders, seeking not simply to restore but to transform. Accountability is multidimensional and transformational.

What are four benefits of victim-offender mediation?

Victim-offender mediation is a form of restorative justice that brings together victims and offenders in a facilitated dialogue to address the harm caused by a crime or wrongdoing. Some benefits of victim-offender mediation include:

1. Increased satisfaction and empowerment for victims: Victim-offender mediation can provide victims with an opportunity to have a voice and be heard, express their feelings and needs, and receive answers to their questions. This can help victims feel validated, empowered, and more satisfied with the outcome of the process.

2. Greater accountability and responsibility for offenders: By meeting with their victims and seeing the impact of their actions, offenders may gain a better understanding of the harm they have caused and feel a greater sense of responsibility and accountability for their actions. This can increase the likelihood of successful rehabilitation and reduce the likelihood of reoffending.

3. Restitution and repair: Victim-offender mediation can provide a framework for repairing the harm caused by the crime or wrongdoing, such as through the payment of restitution, community service, or other forms of compensation. This can help promote a sense of justice and closure for both victims and offenders.

4. Reduced strain on the criminal justice system: By providing an alternative to the traditional criminal justice system, victim-offender mediation can reduce the burden on the court system, save time and resources, and promote greater efficiency and effectiveness in addressing crime and wrongdoing.

In brief:

a): Victim-offender mediation empowers participants,

Victim offender mediation is a process that provides interested victims an opportunity to meet their offender, in a safe and structured setting, and engage in a mediated discussion of the crime. The victim has a chance to speak about the personal dimensions of victimization and loss, while the offender has a chance to express remorse and to explain the circumstances surrounding his/her behavior.

b): challenges misattributions,

c): provides for an exchange of information,

d): and encourages actions aimed at making right.

In a study of 3,142 cases, it was found that offenders who met with their victims were far more likely to successfully complete their restitution obligation (81 percent) than similar offenders who did not participate in mediation (58 percent). Victims who met with their offender in the presence of a trained mediator were more likely to be satisfied (79 percent) with the justice system than similar victims who went through the normal court process (57 percent).

What four preconditions are assumed regarding mediation?

There are several preconditions that are often assumed to be necessary for successful mediation. Four of these preconditions include:

1. Willingness to participate: All parties involved in the dispute must be willing to participate in the mediation process. If one or more parties are not willing to participate, mediation may not be an effective option.

2. Good faith effort: All parties must make a good faith effort to resolve the dispute through mediation. This means that they must be committed to the process and open to finding a mutually acceptable solution.

3. Open communication: Effective communication is essential for successful mediation. All parties must be willing to communicate openly and honestly with each other, and to listen actively to each other's perspectives and concerns.

4. Neutrality and impartiality: The mediator must be neutral and impartial, and not have a stake in the outcome of the mediation. This helps to ensure that the mediator is perceived as fair and trustworthy by all parties, and that the mediation process is seen as a legitimate and credible way to resolve the dispute.

Furthermore,

a): Safety must be assured.

b): Participants must receive the emotional support they need and must be willing to participate.

c): Trained mediators are essential.

d): The timing must be right.

According to Ron Claassen, what three questions must be satisfactorily answered for mediation to be complete?

a): First, has the injustice been recognized and acknowledged? Has the offender owned up to and accepted responsibility for his acts? Have victims' questions been answered? Has the offender had a chance to explain what has been going on in his life?

b): Second, has there been agreement on what needs to be done to restore equity as far as possible?

c): Third, have future intentions been addressed? Does the offender plan to do it again? Is the victim feeling safe? Is there provision for follow-up and for the monitoring of agreements?

In Biblical language, what three categories match the questions above?

a): confession,

James 5:16 says, "Confess your faults one to another, and pray one for another, that ye may be healed." James reminds us that mutual confession and prayer brings healing, both physically and spiritually.

These free us from the heavy burdens (physically and spiritually) of unresolved sin, and removes hindrances to the work of the Holy Spirit.

b): restitution,

This reminds me of the story of Zacchaeus in Luke 19:1-10. Zacchaeus wanted to get right with God, and he saw the need to get right with people too. The law required someone who had stolen to restore the full amount, plus 20%. Zacchaeus cheerfully offered to do far more than the law demanded. Just imagine, considering the way Zacchaeus had made his money, there was probably quite a long list of people waiting for the promised restitution.

c): and repentance.

What are some conditions that might be present, making mediation inappropriate in that case?

a): The fear may be too great, even with support and assurances of safety.

b): Power imbalances between parties may be too pronounced and impossible to overcome.

c): The victim or the offender may be unwilling.

d): The offense may be too heinous or the suffering too severe.

What role could the church play in facilitating rituals as a part of the justice process? By facilitating religious services of lament and healing for those who are interested.

When we as a society punish, we must do so in a context that is just and deserving.

Do you believe there is a place for punishment (pain) in the restorative approach?

If there is room for punishment in a restorative approach, its place would not be central. It would need to be applied under conditions that controlled and reduced the level of pain and in a context where restoration and healing are the goals.

God forgives, but He also allows consequences to follow our actions. For example, see followed later in the life of David because of his sins with Basheba:

- "The sword shall never depart from your house." (2 Samuel 12:10)
- "I will raise up adversity against you from your own house." (2 Sam. 12:11a) David's son Absalom committed treason against his father.
- "I will take your wives before your eyes and give them to your neighbor." (2 Samuel 12:11b)
- "The child who is born to you shall surely die." (2 Samuel 14b) The first-born child of David and Bathsheba died on the seventh day. But their second son was Solomon.

Justice is viewed quite differently when inspected through restorative vs. retributive eyes.:

a) Which one dominates in our justice system today?
Retributive
b) Which one encourages mutuality and cooperation?
Restorative
c) Which one assumes win-lose outcomes?
Retributive
d) Which one ignores relationships?
Retributive
e) Which one matches God's vision for justice?
Restorative

Think of justice as a communication system, designed to send a message. What message does our present criminal justice system send? (Thought questions, answers will vary.): The criminal justice system is designed to deliver "justice for all." This means protecting the innocent, convicting criminals, and providing a fair justice process to help keep order across the country.

CHAPTER XI
WHERE FROM HERE?

Where from Here?

Unlike criminal law, civil law defines wrongs in terms of injuries and liabilities rather than guilt.: That statement is generally true.

Criminal law and civil law are two separate branches of law, each with its own set of rules and procedures. Criminal law deals with offenses that are considered harmful to society as a whole, such as murder, theft, and assault. The focus in criminal law is on punishing the offender for the harm caused to society.

On the other hand, civil law deals with disputes between individuals, organizations, or companies. The primary goal of civil law is to compensate the injured party for the harm suffered, rather than to punish the wrongdoer. In civil law, the plaintiff (the person bringing the lawsuit) must prove that the defendant (the person being sued) caused them harm or injury, and is therefore liable for damages.

In summary, while criminal law focuses on punishing offenders for their actions, civil law is primarily concerned with compensating victims for their injuries and losses. Therefore, civil law defines wrongs in terms of injuries and liabilities, rather than guilt.

Below is a list a few other areas in which civil law differs from criminal law.:

a): Punishment. Civil law allows for degrees of responsibility without defining them in win/lose terms.

b): Since the state is not the victim, the actual participants remain center stage, retaining significant power and responsibility in the process.

c): Procedural safeguards are of less concern,

d): And the relevant facts are less circumscribed.

The application of criminal law is what triggers the retributive paradigm.

In the medieval period, there were two parallel tracks of justice: State Justice and Church Justice. Each track served as a conscience and check on the other.:

Below is the list of some of the strategies and policies of the Community Boards in San Francisco.:

a): Developing neighborhood-based structures for resolving disputes outside the system.

Community Boards offers a nationally recognized course called "The Basics of Mediation." This course introduces core conflict resolution skills in a training designed for managers, human resource professionals, attorneys, ombudsmen, social workers, community mediators and others who must intervene in disputes as part of their work.

They also offer a 40-hour training course called "Basics." Participants gain the knowledge, techniques and skills needed to handle a broad range of disputes. This training is required for those wishing to become volunteer Community Mediators for our Neighborhood Mediation Program.

Basics training topics include:
- Effective communication and active listening skills
- Stages of mediated problem solving
- Balancing power
- Managing a negotiation
- Cultural and gender issues in mediation
- Dealing with strong emotions
- Breaking impasse
- De-escalating anger
- Drafting agreements that work

While California has no Statewide certification process for mediators, "Basics" meets the minimum requirements for most court mediation programs.

b): The programs train people from the community to serve as case workers and as mediators and place a high value on community education and empowerment.

c): Their mediation processes serve as an alternative to civil or criminal courts.

Community Boards is San Francisco's non-profit community resolution center. They help SF residents and businesses resolve a wide variety of conflicts with affordable, multi-lingual, culturally sensitive services. From problems with neighbors, to workplace, business, youth and family disputes, our certified neutral mediators help disputants reach solutions that work.

d): The programs are a means of educating and empowering the community to solve its own problems.

What are some of the drawbacks and issues that have come to light regarding the practice of relying on neighborhood structures as a dispute resolution system, instead of the criminal or civil system?

a): Outcomes may have no uniformity and thus contradict a basic sense of fairness.

b): Informal justice may be reserved primarily for the poor and the powerless, denying them access to other forms of justice.

c): Victims may be given too much power.

d): In the end, the state and the formal justice system may actually receive more, not less, power and legitimation.

In Japan, from the initial police interrogation through the final judicial hearing on sentencing, the vast majority of those accused of criminal offenses:

a): offenses confess, display repentance, negotiate for their victims' pardon

b): submit to the mercy of the authorities.

Three basic features of Japan's system of criminal justice characterize its operations.

- First, the institutions police, government prosecutors' offices, courts, and correctional organs maintain close and cooperative relations with each other, consulting frequently on how best to accomplish the shared goals of limiting and controlling crime.

- Second, citizens are encouraged to assist in maintaining public order, and they participate extensively in crime prevention campaigns, apprehension of suspects, and offender rehabilitation programs.

- Finally, officials who administer criminal justice are allowed considerable discretion in dealing with offenders.

What are two of the factors that lead offenders in Japan to be so willing to confess and take responsibility?

a): The willingness of the offender to acknowledge guilt

b): To express remorse and make compensation to the victim,

Westerners assume that such a lenient response to crime would fail to deter crime.

Do you believe we will see restorative justice established as a full-fledged, system-wide paradigm within the next ten years?

I do not believe, because the retributive paradigm is closely tied to the interests and functions of the modern state. That will have considerable impact on whether the paradigm changes and, if it does, what shape it takes.

What are some things we can be doing, while waiting for the restorative justice paradigm to evolve into a nation-wide system?

a): We must continue to dialogue, to palaver with those who are sympathetic and those who are not.

b): We must test, explore, and develop our vision.

c): We must also become justice farmers, planting our experimental and demonstration plots. We must plant more VOCs, for example, and test new forms and applications of VOC.

As we and others pursue restorative justice "alternatives," what are some of the questions we need to test?

a): What about murder?

b): What about spouse and child abuse? Rape?

c): What are the possibilities and what are the limits?

d): What procedures work and which do not? What safeguards do we need?

What are questions that should be included in a restorative yardstick against which we could measure our efforts?

a): Do they in fact reflect alternative values?

b): Or are they simply alternative technologies?

c): Are they consistent with a restorative focus?

d): Do they move us in that direction?

It should recognize the importance of community involvement and initiative in responding to and reducing crime, rather than leaving the problem of crime to the government alone.

Below is a list of four of the church's responses we have seen develop over the centuries:

a): The first is a strategy of withdrawal. At points the church has tried to insulate itself from the world. The withdrawal strategy is a strategy of unfaithfulness, however, because it ignores the aggressive character of God's justice, which is to be shared with others.

b): A second response is the Constantinian one, a strategy of capitulation.

c): A third strategy was that adopted by the Enlightenment, a strategy that denies the tension between models of justice.

d): a fourth option: to create the new in the midst of the old.

In 1 Corinthians 6:1-8, the Apostle Paul taught the believers that we are to learn to deal with situations as God would, and our training ground is here in this life and in the church. For what reasons did Paul say that Christians should avoid taking their disputes to state courts?

He assumed that the church should develop its own alternative structures to implement covenant justice.

Christians would be unequally yoked in heathen courts of law. The Apostle Paul believed Christians should be fully able to judge their own matters because of our destiny. As we reign with Jesus Christ, we will (in some sense or another) judge the world, and even angels, one day. Christians are being prepared right now for such a glorious destiny,

Retributive justice is deeply embedded in our judicial system, but we can still act on this teaching. In what three areas of our lives can we begin to apply the restorative lens?

While retributive justice is deeply embedded in our judicial system, there are still ways we can begin to apply a restorative lens to other areas of our lives. Here are three areas where restorative justice principles can be applied:

1. Personal relationships: In our personal relationships, we can begin to apply restorative justice principles by focusing on repairing harm and restoring relationships rather than punishing or seeking revenge. This might involve having difficult conversations with loved ones, actively listening to their perspectives and feelings, and working together to find solutions that meet everyone's needs.

2. Workplace conflicts: In the workplace, restorative justice can be applied to resolve conflicts between employees, managers, and teams. Instead of relying on disciplinary action or punishment, restorative justice principles can be used to bring people together to address the root causes of the conflict, repair harm, and build stronger working relationships.

3. Community building: Restorative justice principles can also be applied to build stronger, more connected communities. This might involve organizing community dialogues to address issues like crime, inequality, or discrimination, and working together to find solutions that benefit everyone involved. By focusing on restoring relationships and repairing harm, rather than punishing or blaming individuals, we can build stronger, more resilient communities that are better equipped to address the challenges we face.

Another good answer would be "at school." With the potential of teaching conflict resolution skills to young people, building stronger relationships and providing alternative approaches to discipline, many schools are exploring the use of restorative practices.

School bullying is a good example of a destructive behavior that could be handled this way. Children who bully in school are more likely to continue to use this form of dominating behavior in other contexts, such as close relationships and the workplace. Through effective intervention, we may be able to intervene early and curb this pattern of behavior. For children who are victims of bullying in school, we know the traumatizing effects can lead to depression and suicide. For these children, the challenge is to tap the resources of resilience and empowerment.

After reading this book, has the stratagem through which you view crime and punishment changed at all?

BENEFITS OF RESTORATIVE JUSTICE?

Restorative justice offers several benefits over traditional forms of justice that focus primarily on punishment and retribution. Here are some of the key benefits of restorative justice:

1. Increased victim satisfaction: Restorative justice provides victims with a voice and an opportunity to participate in the justice process. Victims are able to express how the crime or harm has affected them, and have a say in how the offender can make amends. This can lead to greater satisfaction and a sense of closure for the victim.

2. Reduced recidivism: Restorative justice has been shown to reduce recidivism rates, or the likelihood that an offender will commit another crime in the future. This is because restorative justice focuses on addressing the underlying causes of the crime or harm, and providing the offender with opportunities to take responsibility and make amends.

3. Improved community relations: Restorative justice emphasizes the importance of repairing relationships and restoring trust within the community. This can lead to improved community relations and a sense of ownership and responsibility for justice within the community.

4. Cost-effective: Restorative justice can be a cost-effective alternative to traditional forms of justice, which can be expensive and time-consuming. Restorative justice processes such as victim-offender mediation or community conferencing can be less expensive and more efficient than going through the court system.

5. More humane: Restorative justice is a more humane approach to justice, which emphasizes the inherent worth and dignity of all individuals, including both victims and offenders. Restorative justice seeks to promote healing, reconciliation, and restoration, rather than just punishment and retribution.

Accordingly, restorative justice offers a more victim-centered, community-focused, and humane approach to justice, which can lead to greater satisfaction for victims, reduced recidivism rates, improved community relations, and cost-effective outcomes.

CONCLUSION

Is restorative justice better than retributive justice?

Whether restorative justice is better than retributive justice is a matter of perspective and depends on the specific circumstances and goals of a given situation. Both approaches to justice have their strengths and weaknesses, and there may be situations where one approach is more appropriate than the other.

Retributive justice is a traditional approach to justice that emphasizes punishment for wrongdoing. The focus is on punishing offenders and holding them accountable for their actions, with the goal of deterring future criminal behavior. This approach is often seen as necessary to maintain social order and uphold the rule of law.

Restorative justice, on the other hand, is a newer approach that emphasizes repairing harm caused by wrongdoing and restoring relationships between victims and offenders. The focus is on addressing the underlying causes of crime and harm, and promoting healing, forgiveness, and reconciliation. This approach is often seen as more humane and victim-centered.

Some of the potential advantages of restorative justice over retributive justice include:

- Greater victim satisfaction and empowerment
- Reduced recidivism rates
- More efficient use of resources
- Improved community relations
- More humane and compassionate approach

However, restorative justice may not always be appropriate or effective in every situation. There may be cases where punishment is necessary to deter future criminal behavior or to ensure public safety. Additionally, some victims may prefer retributive justice, feeling that it is the only way to obtain justice and closure.

Ultimately, the choice between restorative justice and retributive justice depends on the goals and values of the justice system and the needs and preferences of the individuals involved. In some cases, a hybrid approach that combines elements of both approaches may be the most effective way to achieve justice and promote healing and restoration.

ACKNOWLEDGEMENTS

My special thanks to my dear wife Zipporah, my sons Melvin, and Ian for their constant love and support.

My thanks to my late Father, Reuben Shimba for his consultations, prayers, and editorial work in the preparation of this manuscript.

I also wish to thank my loving mother, Lois Shimba for her prayers, which are a constant source of strength and encouragement to me. My appreciation to my dedicated staff for their assistance with this project.

ABOUT THE AUTHOR

Dr. Maxwell Shimba: A Biography

Dr. Maxwell Shimba is a multifaceted individual whose life journey has been marked by a deep commitment to the fields of restorative justice, literature, religious scholarship, and education. His remarkable contributions span a diverse range of endeavors, making him a prominent figure in these domains.

Restorative Justice Advocate:
Dr. Maxwell Shimba's passion for justice is evident in his role as a dedicated Restorative Justice practitioner. With a profound understanding of this transformative approach to justice, he has actively worked to promote healing, reconciliation, and rehabilitation in the face of conflicts and wrongdoing.

Prolific Author:
An accomplished author, Dr. Shimba has penned numerous books that traverse various disciplines. His literary repertoire includes works on law, religion, finance, and other pertinent subjects. Through his writings, he has not only shared knowledge but also inspired and enlightened countless readers.

Bible Scholar:
Dr. Maxwell Shimba's deep reverence for the Bible is reflected in his status as a Bible scholar. His rigorous study of scripture has allowed him to unravel its profound teachings and share them with others, enriching their understanding of faith and spirituality.

Founder of Shimba Theological Institute:

In his quest to further theological education, Dr. Shimba founded the Shimba Theological Institute in the vibrant city of Manhattan, New York. This institution stands as a testament to his commitment to nurturing the intellectual and spiritual growth of students, imparting knowledge, and fostering a deeper connection with matters of faith.

Teacher and Preacher:

Dr. Maxwell Shimba is not merely an academic but also a dedicated teacher and preacher. Through his teachings and sermons, he imparts wisdom, guidance, and spiritual insights to those who seek a deeper understanding of their faith and the principles that guide their lives.

Dr. Maxwell Shimba's life journey embodies a profound dedication to the principles of justice, faith, education, and the written word. His work continues to impact and influence individuals across various walks of life, making him a beacon of knowledge, inspiration, and positive change in the world.